T.L. OSBORN

THE POWER OF POSITIVE DESIRE

BOOKS BY THE OSBORNS

BELIEVERS IN ACTION—*Apostolic–Rejuvenating*

BIBLICAL HEALING—*Seven Miracle Keys*
4 Visions–60+ yrs. of Proof–324 Merged Bible Vs.

FIVE CHOICES FOR WOMEN WHO WIN
21st Century Options

GOD'S BIG PICTURE—*An Impelling Gospel Classic*

GOD'S LOVE PLAN—*The Awesome Discovery*

HEALING THE SICK—*A Living Classic*

JESUS and WOMEN—*Big Questions Answered*

LIFE–TRIUMPH OVER TRAGEDY (WHY)
A True Story of Life After Death

MIRACLES–*Proof of God's Love*

NEW LIFE FOR WOMEN—*Reality Re-focused*

NEW MIRACLE LIFE NOW
Global Communiqué of The Christian Faith

SOULWINNING-OUTSIDE THE SANCTUARY
A Classic on Biblical Christianity & Human Dignity

THE BEST OF LIFE—*Seven Energizing Dynamics*

THE GOOD LIFE—*A Mini-Bible School–1,467 Ref.*

THE GOSPEL ACCORDING TO T.L. & DAISY
Their Life & World Ministry–510 pg. Pictorial

THE MESSAGE THAT WORKS
T.L.'s Revealing Manifesto on Biblical Faith

THE POWER OF POSITIVE DESIRE
An Invigorating Faith Perspective

THE WOMAN BELIEVER
Awareness of God's Design

WOMAN WITHOUT LIMITS
Unmuzzled—Unfettered—Unimpeded

WOMEN & SELF-ESTEEM
Divine Royalty Unrestrained

YOU ARE GOD'S BEST
Transforming Life Discoveries

OSBORN
P U B L I S H E R S

USA HQ:
OSBORN INTERNATIONAL
P.O. Box 10, Tulsa, OK 74102 USA

T.L. OSBORN, FOUNDER & PRES.
LADONNA OSBORN, VICE-PRES. & CEO

Tel: 918/743-6231
Fax: 918/749-0339   E-Mail: OSFO@aol.com
www.OSBORN.ORG

Canada: Box 281, Adelaide St. Post Sta., Toronto M5C 2J4
England: Box 148, Birmingham B3 2LG
(A Registered Charity)

iii

BIBLE QUOTATIONS IN THIS BOOK MAY BE PER-
SONALIZED, PARAPHRASED, ABRIDGED OR CONFORMED
TO THE *PERSON* AND *TENSE* OF THEIR CONTEXTUAL AP-
PLICATION IN ORDER TO FOSTER CLARITY AND INDI-
VIDUAL ACCEPTANCE. VARIOUS LANGUAGE TRANSLA-
TIONS AND VERSIONS HAVE BEEN CONSIDERED. BIBLICAL
REFERENCES ENABLE THE READER TO COMPARE THE PAS-
SAGES WITH HIS OR HER OWN BIBLE.

THE AUTHOR

2005-04

ISBN 0-87943-141-5
Copyright 2005 by LaDonna C. Osborn
Printed in the United States of America
All Rights Reserved

CONTENTS

SECTION V—PERSPIRE

SECTION VI—ACQUIRE

SECTION VII—INSPIRE

DEDICATED

To THE MEMORY of Daisy, my beloved
wife, co-founder of OSFO International
and of its soulwinning ministries worldwide, associate minister in sharing Jesus
and His life with millions face to face in
over eighty nations; and whose collabo-
ration, counsel and creative editing, have
been indispensable to the preparation of
this book.

T.L. OSBORN

Dear Friend:

THE POWER OF POSITIVE DESIRE is a dynamic force that, if understood, will lift you to the realization of a happy, forceful, healthy and successful lifestyle.

I think I am qualified to help you discover this force, in its **positive** sense.

I met my wife, Daisy Marie Washburn, when I was only 17 and she was only 16. One year later we were married. At 20 and 21, we were missionaries in India. At 23 and 24, audiences of from 10,000 to 25,000 were coming to hear us teach. We were privileged to experience over 53 years of happiness, love and international ministry together before her demise in 1995.

In over 80 nations, our audiences have numbered from 20,000 to 300,000 — in stadiums, ball parks, race tracks and out on open fields where people of all religions, creeds and persuasions can freely attend.

We believe that the only authentic message from God is **good** news.

Hinduism and Buddhism accept conditions of poverty, unhappiness, inadequacy, sickness, insignificance or inferiority as the fate of the gods.

Religion or Good News

When Christianity is reduced to just another religion, it is not very different. The "religion" which pharisaical tradition has formed from Christianity is rooted in pious, medieval theology and has lost its **good** news.

Is it logical for true believers in God and in the Bible to bow in hopeless submission to demoralizing and depressing conditions? Can that increase spiritual qualities?

Religion* seems to inevitably exact some kind of contrition or self-reproach of its adherents.

God believes in you, values you and esteems you so highly that He created you just a little lower than Himself, then decked your world with every conceivable treasure and beauty for your health, happiness, success and fulfillment.

He created this fabulous world to be utilized by those whom He created in His own image.

Is it a generally accepted idea that humanity has sinned, therefore people must now pay for their transgressions by physical suffering, deprivation and the indignities of impoverishment?

---

*I mean the profusion of restrictive, medieval teachings emanating from misinterpretations of the Bible which breed fear, condemnation and guilt, instead of faith, love and mercy; which demoralize, discourage and disparage the human spirit instead of uplift, encourage and enhance the self-esteem and the good creative potential in people.

The Bible is clear about the fruits of sin. But the **good** news is that God never quit on us, even when we blundered. Rather, He was so fond of us that He gave His Son to redeem us from *our* sins by suffering *our* punishment, in *our* name—so that we may be free forever of guilt, condemnation and judgment.

The Message That Lifts People

If we must continue to cower, to suffer, to accept inferiority and to live in self-reproach, then the death of Jesus Christ is of little benefit to us while we live on this earth.

Archaic theology misses the point of the **Good News.** The Bible message is to lift people instead of to put them down. It announces forgiveness instead of condemnation. It helps people discover the good life of health, happiness, success and self-esteem, instead of berating them as Joshua Liebman says most Western religions do: **"Atone you miserable human worm! Smite yourself with the rod of punishment. Lacerate your guilty soul ...else you be not worthy in the sight of God."**

THE POWER OF POSITIVE DESIRE is written to motivate you to reject mediocrity and to experience excellence.

Desire Is an Empire

When understood and directed **positively,** desire is a powerful force inside a person. As you read this book, this creative energy which may have been neutralized in you by prejudiced religious influence, will be freed and you will begin to soar.

When it happens inside you, the circumstances and conditions around you will conform positively. God will be released to materialize His abundant goodness in your life.

I am not lauding an unbalanced view of material gain. Your attitude might be like ours has been. We have never chosen material prosperity. **But we believe that God deposited material wealth in this planet for the blessing and the use of His children who do His will on earth.**

God Gave Us Our Choice

When we were young, we had a profound spiritual experience during a period of prayer for God's guidance.

In a remarkable way, the Lord said to us: **You can have a rich and successful ministry in the United States. You will prosper materially, and enjoy life's richest and best. I created it, and it is my will for you to enjoy earth's material abundance as well as my spiritual success, in unlimited form.**

Or, you may not aspire to material wealth, but you may go and share my abundance with the peoples of the world. If you do this, you will

manage millions of dollars for the good of humanity worldwide, and you will still live like royalty and have everything you ever desire.

That is what we chose. Every material blessing entrusted to us has been devoted to helping people around the world to discover God's goodness.

We raised our children and lived our lives in nations of the world. Huts, cabins, motels and hotels have been our mansions.

Oxcarts, taxis, trains, boats, ships and planes have been our chariots.

Marketplaces, shade trees, sidewalk stalls, cafes and restaurants have been our banquet halls.

The landscapes, the hillsides, the deserts, the rivers, the parks and colorful beauty around the world have been our private gardens.

The blue sky and the star-spangled canopy of the heavens have constituted our cathedral for teaching the masses.

We are royalty. We are rich. Our wealth is inside us, and nothing on this earth can take away the lifestyle of dignity, divine royalty and self-esteem from us.

Golden Discovery

When we encourage you to look up and to reach for excellence, we do not mean to exaggerate the importance of material gain. We mean to emphasize **your** importance as a creation of God.

This book will be a **golden discovery of your own self-wealth.** The result of that spiritual self-wealth in you is as certain to produce physical and material wealth in and around you, as wheat, planted in good soil, is certain to produce wheat.

All I can say now is — WOW! You and I are going to make a terrific journey together. You are headed for the top. **From this moment, promise never again to think of yourself as ordinary.** You are too vital to God to demean what He esteems.

Everything is in you to build your **empire of desire.**

We love you and we shall be praying for you as you read. My daughter, LaDonna and I live to lift people because that is what God wants. So, let's go.

LaDonna Osborn

INTRODUCTION

God has gifted each person with a divine power that is unique in creation, the power of *desire*. This providential, energizing force—when understood—unleashes humanity's potential for good, and allows the supernatural purposes of God to be expressed in ways that bring healing and hope to a hurting world.

Often when people think of *desire*, their mind focuses only on material things, such as financial prosperity or individual happiness. Many secular and religious books have been written to guide people in their search for material wealth and happiness, for success and peace, and for life-purpose and fulfillment.

What is unique about THE POWER OF POSITIVE DESIRE, written by my father? Why did this book need to be written? Why has it answered some of the difficult questions asked by people of many nations and cultures who view the "Americanized" message of personal success and achievement as relevant only to the West? Why will it transform your thinking about your own desires and your own purpose in life?

Too often Christians have been taught that *desires* are evil or carnal and that personal desires are opposed to the highest ideals of Bible-based living. This erroneous concept has caused many Christ-centered men and women to live in doubt concerning the desires of their hearts; to resist God-ideas that are intended to bring blessing and hope; and has burdened them with unnecessary guilt and condemnation. While it is true that self-centered ambition and negative desire is contrary to the redeemed lifestyle, it is also true that God created within human persons the capacity for positive desire. The purpose of this book is to activate the positive desire that is within you so that you can experience a greater sense of your connection with God and an increased awareness of your own potential for good toward others.

Our lives and ministries are centered in the Person of Jesus Christ and in what He has made available to those who believe in Him, and who trust in what He has provided through his life, death, burial and resurrection. These provisions are available to all people. The truths and concepts in THE POWER OF POSITIVE DESIRE are based on the principles of divine scripture, the Word of God. All truly biblical teachings will apply to any person, regardless of gender, color, race, or social class. Whether you are living in a city in the

United States or in a village of Russia, God's plan for you is for your GOOD. He desires your happiness, peace, dignity, fulfillment and material blessing.

The biblical message of positive desire is not exclusively for the more prosperous nations or people. God's plan for success, peace, happiness and purpose is for everyone because His redemption plan includes ALL who believe on Christ.

During my lifetime of travels and ministry among people of so many different cultures and circumstances, I have witnessed God's inexhaustible love for people. Even the most isolated and forgotten of humanity are important to God the Creator who reveals Himself to us through Jesus Christ. The biblical message of positive desire is God's reminder that He wants to partner with human persons, in every area of their lives. I have witnessed the most unlikely men and women completely transformed by the loving presence and life of Christ. Former beggars have become dignified business people. Insecure failures have become confident voices for progress in their communities. Simple people with limited resources have become financiers of enormous gospel enterprises for hurting people.

As you read this book, be alert for the voice of God speaking to you. These truths will take you beyond the realm of limited secular success. They will lift your spirit to a new level of awareness of God in your thinking, your believing and in your living. You will discover the untapped reservoir of your own divine potential to experience life to the fullest, in relationship and in partnership with the God of all abundance...THE POWER OF POSITIVE DESIRE.

LaDonna C. Osborn,
Doctor of Ministry (D.Min.)

Chapter I

LIBERATED
FROM LIMITATIONS

MICHELANGELO BOUGHT a chunk of marble which others esteemed inferior. When asked why, he replied:

"Because there is an angel locked in that marble, and I must set it free."

When I think of any one who is imprisoned by a sense of inferiority because of race, color, social, academic or economic status, or when I see someone who is lonely, abused, discouraged or afraid, I know that inside that individual is a **super person** whom I must find the way to set free.

The Big Idea

I gave a television address on the subject:

Boo the Taboos,
Choose the Glad News.

Religions dwarf minds, make beggars out of princes, robots out of creators and turn freedom into subjugation by their thesaurus of "no-nos" and "don't dos."

All the time, God is saying:

*Things beyond your **seeing**, your **hearing** and your **imagining**, are prepared for those who love me; and I have revealed them.* 1Cor.2:9-10NEB

God wants you…

To **desire** His best,

To **inquire** of His way,

To **admire** His provisions,

To **aspire** to His blessings,

To **require** His abundance,

To **perspire** (if need be) to attain His resources,

To **acquire** His lifestyle,

To **inspire** His posterity.

God wants you liberated from all limitations imposed upon you by any person, condition or system. You need nobody's permission to be healthy, wealthy, happy and successful. God wants to free your wings of desire so they can lift you to new frontiers and new fortunes.

God only has **one idea** about you, and He has never changed His mind. His idea is: To share His life and His abilities with you, to make you happy, healthy, talented and prosperous, to make you into **a super human person.**

Jesus summed up His Father's will for **you** when He said:

*I came that **you** might have life — abundance of it.*[Jn.10:10]

Transcend Mediocrity

As your wings of desire are freed to soar, you will discover fresh new faith blossoming in you for GOOD things, HAPPY times, HEALTHY living, BIG dreams—abundance, success and contentment.

Religion says "NO. You are not worthy—not good enough. You must be humble and patient. Be content with your fate. The best may be for others, but not for you. It might make you bad or proud."

This book in your hands proves that you are destined to see your **desires** become realities.

You will discover the magnitude of God's glad news and you will transcend mediocrity and commonality.

You will blossom into the excellence for which God designed you.

No good thing will he withhold from those who walk uprightly.[Psa.84:11]

God has now begun a good work in you; he will complete it. Phil.1:6

*Delight yourself in him and he shall give you the **desires** of your heart.* Psa.37:4

Chapter 2

SETTING THE ANGEL FREE

LET YOUR WINGS of desire soar so you can explore the good life God offers anyone who is free to see and to be a new "she" or a new "he."

There is nothing but goodness in him. Psa.92:15LB

God is good, and he loves goodness. Psa.11:7LB

When you discover how good God is, you will discover why you can be good.

When you believe in God, you can believe in you — the you He created.

When you understand His love-plan to ransom you so that He can sculpture you and restore you to His image again, tremendous self-confidence and self-wealth will be born in you.

The Stuff for Excellence

If God be for you, who can be against you? Rom.8:31

That is to say…

When God conforms you to His ideal,
Who can deform what He has made real.

His material in you is the stuff for excellence — if He can free you, then inspire you to spread your wings of **desire** and to fly.

His idea is...

> *To set the angel in you free,*
> *And let you gain all you can see.*

By the time you finish reading this book, you will sense a new freedom; you will have a **new birth** of **new worth**.

You will forget how you used to think in the restricted, judgmental pews of pious nitpicking.

You will climb to a new plateau.

> *You will then pursue,*
>   *The boundless view*
> *Of the renewed you,*
>   *That you never knew.*

> *You will bid adieu*
>   *To the old taboo,*
> *To the gray mildew*
>   *On left-over stew.*

First: **You will INQUIRE** about God's dream and His plan for you, to see if He truly wants you happy, healthy, successful and fulfilled.

Second: **You will ADMIRE** the abundant goodness and overwhelming liberality that God has shown toward you.

Third: **You will ASPIRE** to the good life of excellence as you discover God's emotions at work within you.

Fourth: You will REQUIRE God's best as you recognize His plan and see how vital you are to it.

Fifth: You may PERSPIRE as you stake new claims and make new gains, despite devout resistance and negative insistence.

Sixth: You will ACQUIRE the blessings and the esteem of God's new lifestyle as you act on new discoveries.

Seventh: You will INSPIRE your world around you as your riches and confidence overflow to bless others.

Each section of this book will lift you higher as you are chiseled free from the block of sectarian conformity, and shaped by the master artist into the dynamic person He created you to be.

Chapter 3

BLOSSOM WITH GOD'S IDEAS

LIFTED BY THE POWER OF POSITIVE DESIRE, you discover the sustaining force that motivates you through wind or storm, through dark nights and stark plights, through tough times or rough climbs, through cynicism and ostracism, until you, like the person in Christ's parable, find *the pearl of great price.*[Mat.13:46]

> *The old ideas*
> *Of miser-mediocrity,*
> *Bow to bold ideas*
> *Of wiser generosity.*

When you glance back, after you have gained this knowledge you will realize that...

> *You refused*
> *The mildewed stew,*
> *You transfused*
> *The renewed you.*

You will be amazed at the changes in your life as your attitude blossoms with God's ideas. You will no longer be blocked by the traditions of the past or mummified by medieval concepts. You will be so glad that you **inquired**, 'til you **admired** and then **acquired** what you **desired**. You will say with a grin:

> I don't plop in a slot
>   Nor flop in a squat,
> I'll opt for the top —
>   A new lot; a new crop.

New Horizons

You will flourish in this fresh frontier, as you welcome new ideas that will push you toward new horizons.

> Refuse the refrain of the status quo.
> Choose the domain of the faith-pro.

The Lord said to a woman whom everyone else was ready to put down: *I do not condemn you.*[Jn.8:11]

He said, *I did not come to condemn you, but to save you.*[Jn.3:17]

He is saying to you right now:

> "Regardless of your past,
>   I still believe in you.
> Be fearless; you're not trash.
>   I've come to live in you."

He always believes in people. He proves it by His willingness to trust people to carry out His plans.

Jesus said, *Whoever comes to me, I will in no way reject you.*[Jn.6:37] To encourage people to reach out to Him for His blessings in life, He said, *Blessed*

are they who hunger and thirst; they shall be filled.
Mat.5:6

What do you want? Riches, honor, love, success or recognition?

Most people do not know what they want. They are so occupied with the struggle for existence that they cannot focus with persistence.

Instead...

> *They jog along in a strut,*
> *Or plod along in a rut.*

Because...

> *They are bored.*
> *It is the same routine.*
> *They never score.*
> *They have no dream.*

Chapter 4

FEED YOUR BRAIN
AND SEED YOUR GAIN

NEW THOUGHTS of God's abundance and of
His goodness...

> *Will fill your mind,*
> *And fire your desire;*
>
> *They will skill your climb,*
> *And inspire you higher.*

Desiring is choosing...

> *Which route you will take.*
> *Which choice you will make.*
> *Which taboo you will shake.*
> *Which restraint you will break.*
> *Which desire you will stake.*
> *Which dream you will wake.*

We have lived to inspire in people THE POSITIVE
POWER OF DESIRE for God's best. We reach out for
seed-ideas which will be fresh enough to hold at-
tention long enough to plant them in people's
minds and spirits.

I was contemplating the miracles which can be
experienced by those receptive to good seeds — or

the disappointments encountered by those who reject them, and a clever little poem popped into my mind. I suppose God uses a bit of wit, to infuse us with new grit, so at the risk of sounding frivolous, here are the words:

> *If you bone-dry your brain,*
> *   You will bon-zai your gain;*
> *But if you satisfy your brain,*
> *   You will magnify your gain.*
>
> *When you signify your brain,*
> *   You will dignify your gain;*
> *But if you nullify your brain,*
> *   You will mortify your gain.*
>
> *What you specify to your brain,*
> *   You will testify in your gain;*
> *But if you french-i-fry your brain,*
> *   You will scrimpy-tie your gain.*

SECTION I

INQUIRE

BE NOT AFRAID to assert boldly: "I **want** this, and I am going to **have** it! It is my rightful heritage, and I **demand** it!"

If we do not **INQUIRE** about life's blessings and its laws, we will never discover them. Examine God's dream. What was His idea for the people He created in His likeness?

Is it right for unbelievers to seek the good life, but wrong for believers to have material success? Is it wrong for a bird to fly, for a fish to swim?

THE POWER OF POSITIVE DESIRE springs from the **awareness** or the **knowledge** of who you are, of what God thinks of you, of what He provided for you and of what He planned for you in life.

Chapter 5

THINKING FREE

BY WHAT LAW do those who **have** get more, while those who **have not** continue doing without?

Is life cut out that way? Is that destiny or fate at work?

Should the resources of this world be equally distributed by governments?

Many think Jesus made a strange statement:

*To those who have, more will be given and they will have great plenty; but from those who have not, even the little they have will be taken away.*Mat.13:12-13LB

The Gift of a Strong Will

Robert Collier made a powerful statement about this issue. Talking about the **desire** and **will** of people, he explained that they usually accept their lot and are content with it. But he added, "This is not nature's way." He says that we have all been given the capacity for **strong desire** and the gift of a **will** that pushes us **to get what we really want in life.**

He then said about the LAW of nature (or God's system): "When the **many** use the LAW, the **few** will cease to be the sole possessors of the good things in life. Therefore, be not afraid to stand boldly out, crying: 'I **want** this, and I am going to **have** it! It is my rightful heritage, and I **demand it!**'"

Should we allow ourselves to **desire** better things in life? How much? What? Why? And if so, when does desire become lust, envy, greed or covetousness?

A great Christian gentleman, F.F. Bosworth, said to me years ago: "Always desire what God desires, and desire it for the same reason He desires it, then His Holy Spirit will work with you to achieve what you want."

Begin to Live

When we recognize ourselves as God's creation, and allow Him to live in us as He originally dreamed, then **our desires are His desires being expressed in and through us.**

To share God's desires, we must first inquire and discover what He wants.

Hosea said, *People are destroyed for lack of knowledge.*[Hos.4:6]

Solomon said, *Leave behind foolishness and begin to live.*[Prov.9:6LB] *Let me show you common sense. I have important information for you. Search* [knowledge]

34

and you shall find unending riches, honor, justice and righteousness which are God's to distribute.[Prov.8:4-7,17-18LB]

God's idea for us is that we use our ears to hear His laws about success; that we use our eyes to observe what works; that we learn the secrets of achievement which are available to anyone.

Don't Bow to Fate
But Vow to Rate

Hindu beggars wail and chant, day after day, in the same gutter, at the roadside or same market gate, until they die. They believe in the fate of their gods; that they are born to beg; that their worst sin would be to **dare to desire anything better.** They cower, crawl, cry and die in emptiness, shame and uselessness, amidst a world of PLENTY that surrounds them.

No human being was ever born for mediocrity, non-productivity, poverty or shame.

But we must **INQUIRE.** We must look, search, observe, learn—and discover.

Jesus said: *Ask, seek, knock.*[Mat.7:7]

If we do not **INQUIRE** about life's blessings and its laws, we will never discover them.

Jesus said that the reason those who have not, lose even what they have, is because, *they hear, but do not understand; they look, but do not see!*[Mat.13:14LB]

To understand the good life and God's laws by which we acquire it, our minds must be uncluttered by religious prejudice and bigotry, unmanipulated by pharisaic reservations and pious intimidations.

A Long Happy Life

We must be willing to think free. Solomon appealed to people to *learn to be wise and to develop good judgment and common sense! I cannot overemphasize this point,*[Prov.4:5LB] he added.

He said, *You will have a long happy life. It will lead you to great honor, and place a beautiful crown upon your head. It will lead you to real living — to the wisest life there is.*[Prov.4:4-13LB]

That is a formidable and attractive offer.

> *A long happy life.*
> *Great honor…a beautiful crown.*
> *A long good life.*
> *The wisest life there is.*
> *Real living.*

Do you dare to DESIRE these things?

Were you born to exist without these blessings?

Are the odds stacked against you?

Does fate determine your state in life?

❀

Chapter 6

PENURY OR PROSPERITY

IF EVERYONE would use God's laws, discipline themselves and go for life's best, the "privileged" **few** would cease to monopolize the good life. The so-called "underprivileged" **majority** would transform themselves by God's principles and the successful life would be shared by the **many**.

Religions say, "Beware! Material affluence—or even sufficiency may corrupt or spoil people."

This demeaning assault on Christian minds began during the Dark Ages.

An unprejudiced study of early Christianity reveals the practice of positive faith for God's abundant lifestyle. **They prospered and they were generous.**

Doctrines to Sanctify Poverty

Then Constantine's acceptance of Christ popularized Christianity. Following this epoch, a dominating church hierarchy evolved to control business, science, education and religion. Astute ecclesiastical leaders manipulated public wealth until the religious system monopolized financial control, and the people were reduced to poverty through tolls and taxes.

The masses became restless in their subservient role and asserted their claim to a better life. That was when financial experts of the church hierarchy consorted with the clergy to invent doctrines which would sanctify poverty and thus pacify the peasantry.

Invoking God, they brainwashed the people who were not allowed to read the Bible. Their mischievous dictums advocated:

** That material poverty fosters spiritual humility;

** That prosperity or the good life motivates arrogance, pride and sinful living;

** That ordinary people are not qualified to manage material wealth without being infected by its potential malignancy.

To this day, many church dogmas, handed down from that medieval period, still proliferate, sanctifying poverty and stigmatizing prosperity.

Bible teachings intended to discourage the perverted love of money, have been twisted into threatening doctrines that material gain produces arrogance and invites damnation.

Neutered Creativity

Religion has incessantly neutralized creativity by persuading people that to **desire** the better life is to "covet" or "lust" or "envy" the forbidden fruit.

Without what Solomon called *common sense and good judgment*, the "sanctified" inferiority syndrome will go on circumscribing the lives of millions who, if freed from these recriminating prejudices, have the "stuff" in them to rise out of commonality and turn their dreams into reality.

INQUIRE about God's ideas for you. Dare to be a thinker. Reexamine God's dream. What was His idea for the people He created in His likeness?

After Satan tempted Adam and Eve to question God's word and to disobey Him, there was no more basis for life on His level. But did God abandon His people project? What about the incalculable price He paid to repurchase you from slavery?

Created for the Good Life

Why did God pay so much to restore you to Him?

The answer must be: That is how much He thinks you are worth!

If God values you that much, would **you** not be the reason for the abundance of His creation all around you? Who else would it have been created for?

Is it **right** for unbelievers to seek the good life, to apply God's laws of success and to achieve their goals?

Is it **wrong** for someone with faith in God to be blessed materially?

Should believers in God venerate their poverty, ignore God's success laws, and deify their misery? Or is that a hangover from the epoch of ecclesiastical lords and "unworthy" peasants?

Is it wrong for a bird to fly, for a fish to swim? Should your eyes feast on the beauty of nature? Should you be condemned for desiring the good life?

Your Rightful Domain

Many religious books conspire to condemn as sinful any desire for material blessing.

Psychological books often confuse the problem further by doing little more than dividing people into categories of emotional subnormality.

So people withdraw within themselves and die in insignificance, loneliness, depression and confusion.

All they need to free their angel's wings and to soar, is to see themselves as God's creation and to see this earth's abundance as their rightful domain.

God told Adam and Eve, *I have given you every herb bearing seed, which is upon the face of the earth, and every tree in which is the fruit of a tree yielding seed; every beast of the earth, every fowl of the air, everything in which there is life.*^{Gen.1:29-30}

Later the record mentions everything that is *pleasant to the eye and good for meat.*^{Gen.2:9} Then the list includes *gold, bedellium,* and *onyx stone.*^{Gen.2:11-12} The forests, the rivers, the gardens, the mineral, animal, fowl and fish life, were all created for people to enjoy, to admire, to possess and to utilize.

When Adam and Eve violated this rich trust, disobeyed God's law, and were consequently separated from the good life, **the positive power of desire became a negative force for greed, envy and lust.**

But now that God so loved us that He gave His Son to redeem us back to Him, if we accept this gift of love and believe that Jesus Christ took *our* judgment and justified us as though we had never sinned, we are restored to God and He comes back to live in us. **The wealth, beauty and abundance of this world become our domain again.**

Our Right to Choose and Win

Our freedom to act upon our desires and to decide and choose the things we believe are good and right for God and for people, is the open door to our success in life. If the wrong passions are fostered, they become the catalyst for our own self-destruction.

We must not allow religious scruples to so exaggerate the unconverted passions of envy, greed and lust that we subjugate THE POWER OF POSITIVE DESIRE for good and useful values in life.

We must never limit our desires, stifle our imagination, strangle our faith, smother our enthusiasm, restrain our endurance, asphyxiate our aspiration, extinguish our exuberance, restrict our achievement or suppress our improvement.

Chapter 7

COMMON SENSE
OF ABUNDANCE

Every BABY is born with **desire**.

1ST Every baby's first cry is its drive and its desire being expressed.

2ND Then as those children reach out for life, their hands get spatted. Confusion, intimidation and insecurity develop.

3RD As they grow, religion infects their attitude with the syndrome of guilt, shame and the loss of self-esteem.

4TH Discouraged by the condemnation of their desires, they become inhibited and withdrawn.

5TH Convinced that God says "NO!", they settle for mediocrity and the fun is gone. The light goes out. They ask in dismay, "Where's the joy in living?"

This is not God's idea for you.

All in the Family

Jesus came with a daring, new message to lift people to God. He brought new hope to humanity and talked of God and people as the Father and His family.

He urged people to have *faith in God.*Mk.11:22

He taught them not to cower and beg like pagans, not to accept their inferior lot in life as though some deity had dealt them a bad hand, but to bestir themselves, to lift up their heads and to look around at God's abundance and at His power; to *ask, seek, knock;* that *everyone that asks receives.*Mat.7:7-8 He was teaching them THE POSITIVE POWER OF DESIRE.

To make His *common sense* point, He reasoned:

If a child asks its parent for bread, will it be given a stone? Or if it asks for a fish, will it be given a serpent?

If you know to give good things to your children, is it not logical that your Father in heaven will give good things to his children who ask for them? Mat.7:9-11

It makes good sense to understand that God created the abundant goodness on this earth for you and for me. He created us with the instinct and **desire** to reach out for, to seek, to ask for that abundant goodness.

Desire the Best

Jesus Christ came with good ideas.

He came to show and to do God's will on earth.

He saw people like His Father saw them. He believed in them and lifted them. He forgave them and planted in them self-esteem.

He transformed a prostitute into a lady, a leper into a healthy community example, a naked maniac into a gentleman.

He said **good things** are for people.

He taught **good news**.

Be free to **desire** the best. It is meant for you.

THE POWER OF POSITIVE DESIRE arouses...
> *Your will to get,*
> *Your will to decide,*
> *Your will to count the cost,*
> *Your will to take the risk,*
> *Your will to persevere,*
> *Your will to try and to fail,*
> *Your will to pay for your failure,*
> *Your will to start again,*
> *Your will to bear responsibility,*
> *Your will to not quit,*
> *Your will to succeed,*
> *Your will to share,*
> *Your will to lift your world.*

THE POWER OF POSITIVE DESIRE is **good**.

But it springs from the **awareness** or the **knowledge** of who you are, of what God thinks of you, of what He provided for you, of what He planned for you in life.

Faith comes by hearing the word of God. Rom.10:17

Faith is your desire turned heavenward.

Prayer is your desire expressed Godward.

Action, based on knowledge, is your desire hooked up to a method for achievement. It is asserting your right to **be**, to **have**, to **do** whatever you desire that is good for God, for you and for people.

Chapter 8

INQUIRE AND DISCOVER

JESUS ANNOUNCED an unlimited lifestyle.

Almost everything He said or did was contrary to what the religious system advocated. The very idea of GOOD news **was an affront to their sectarian, parsimonious outlook on life.**

Jesus said, *the kingdom of God is in you.*^{Lu.17:21}

He gave importance to people.

*All things whatever **you desire**,*^{Mk.11:24} you can have them. That was what He taught.

Where did the idea come from that we are to be content with nothing?

The Greatest Teacher

Jesus explained that the *Gentiles* ^{Mat.6:32} (those without faith in the true God) constantly seek and search after what they can **eat** or **drink** or **wear**.

He implied that they would always struggle for the mere basics of life and never have enough.

But as for God's children with faith in Him, He said, *Your Father knows you need all of these things.* Mat.6:32 In other words, all of the good things for this life have been created and placed here **for those who believe in God and serve Him.** When you understand God's plan, you should *never want* [for] **any good thing.** Psa.34:10

David wrote: *The Lord is my shepherd, I shall **not** want.* Psa.23:1

The apostle Paul desired, that *you may* **lack nothing.** 1Th.4:12

Desire and Discover God's Kingdom

Jesus taught: *Seek first* [1] *the kingdom of God,* [2] *and His righteousness, then* **all of these things** *shall be* **added** *to you.* Mat.6:33

ALL OF THESE THINGS—all you can eat and drink and wear and enjoy and use, is meant to be yours in this life. **On what condition?**

Jesus said to **inquire**—or **seek** until you understand (1) *God's kingdom* in you, and (2) *God's righteousness* in you. In other words, (1) **His** family domain, and (2) **your** right standing in it.

The kingdom of God **in you** Lu.17:21 simply means that God's realm or domain or center of action or dwelling or lifestyle is headquartered **in you**.

    a. God created this world.

    b. God owns this world.

c. God has the right to rule this world.

d. God wills to rule this world through people like you and me.

e. That is God's kingdom on earth.

The book of Genesis explains that God created this world and all that is in it. Then He created man and woman *in his own likeness and image,* and placed them here to *have dominion* over it, to *replenish* it, to *be fruitful and to multiply* or reproduce of their kind. God said to them, I *have given it to you.*[Gen.1:27-31]

They had the Creator's authority to utilize everything good on this earth for the health, happiness, success and fulfillment of this dream.

On God's Level

God came and talked with Adam and Eve in the garden. They were friends and partners.

David said, *God created people a little lower than himself.*[Psa.8:5] [King James Version says, *a little lower than the angels,* but the Hebrew word is *Elohim* or *God.*] *Then he crowned them with glory and honor and gave them dominion over the works of his hands and put all things under their feet.*[Psa.8:5-6]

God created people to share His realm. **That is His kingdom in people.**

God's plan was based on mutual integrity. His word was His bond to Adam and Eve. Their word was their bond to Him.

But God's enemy, Satan, was jealous of His plan to let the people He created share His dominion.

That was the position Satan envied. As an angel, *he wanted to be equal with God.* [Isa.14:12-14]

So Satan came to Adam and Eve, assumed a role of authority and deceived them.

They believed Satan's lie [Gen.3:4] instead of what God had said [Gen.2:17] and consequently forfeited their position of trust. [Gen.3:16-20]

No longer qualified to live on God's level, they were separated from His domain [Gen.3:23-24] and succumbed to the subservient role of slavery under their chosen master, Satan.

How could they recover their position?

They could not. They had sinned. God's law decreed that *sin would produce death,* [Eze.18:4,20; Rom.6:23] and their sin infected all generations that followed.

*Whereas, sin entered into the world, and **death by sin**; death passed upon all persons, because all have sinned.* [Rom.5:12]

Love Had an Idea

But God is love. [1Jn.4:8] He loved us too much to let us all die for our sins. He said, *I have no pleasure in the death of those who die.* [Eze.18:23,32; 2Pet.3:9]

So, Love had an idea. It was to redeem us by offering a perfect, sinless substitute to assume our guilt and *our* punishment, in *our* name.

Jesus Christ willingly assumed the penalty of our sins so that we could be **restored** to God and **justified** before Him **as though we had never sinned.** Jn.3:16; Rom.5:6,8

He bore our sins in his own body on the cross, that we, being dead to sins, should live to righteousness. 1Pet.2:24 (Be sure to read my book, GOD'S LOVE PLAN.)

After Jesus bore *our* judgment, *God raised him from the dead.* Ac.2:32; 3:15 Then He sent His followers to tell **everyone in the world** Mk.16:15 what He had done for them. He promised that each one who would believe this Good News would be reborn with new life from God. They would be restored to His family again. Jn.1:12; 2Cor.5:17; Jn.3:16,36; 1Jn.5:12

Since no sin can be punished twice and no debt is paid twice, we are no longer guilty before God, and we can never be condemned or judged again for our past sins. Jn.5:24; Rom.8:1 Now Christ's righteousness is credited to our account. 2Cor.5:21 There is nothing against us anymore—no condemnation, no guilt, no judgment or penalty to fear.

We are **justified**. It is **just-as-if-I'd** never sinned. Now we live with **God's life again**, imparted to us by a miracle of His love. Rom.6:4; Gal.2:20

All we have to do is to **believe** that Jesus Christ took our place and assumed our judgment.

Now God can come home to us and we can come home to Him again. His Holy Spirit can live in us. We can be born again. His life can become *our* life again. **That is God's kingdom in us.**

Jesus said: *Seek first the kingdom of God.*Mat.6:33 *Seek* that relationship first.

Desire and Discover God's Righteousness

The second principle for you to *seek*, in order for *all of these things to be added to you,*Mat.6:33 is **God's righteousness.**

What does *righteousness* mean?

It means **the ability to stand in the presence of God without a sense of guilt, inferiority or condemnation.**

We can do that only when we understand how Jesus Christ paid *our* debt, took *our* sins, assumed *our* guilt, suffered *our* penalty and died in *our* place, in *our* name, so that we can be **redeemed, restored** to God and **justified** before Him as though no sin had ever existed in *our* lives.

God is saying: When you (1) inquire and understand **me and my domain**, and when you (2) inquire and understand **you and your right standing in my realm**, then your life will be like I originally dreamed for you: *all of these things will be added to you.*Mat.6:33

He is saying, "It is my will for you to have dominion in this life on earth, to live in abundance, and to carry out my dream of helping others discover this life."

Chapter 9

GOD'S TRUST IN US

GOD'S ABUNDANCE in this world was never intended for the **few** to monopolize. It is created for His people to enjoy and to utilize for the good and glory of themselves, of God and of others.

But there are laws which God has made a part of this universe. All who apply them can become achievers and possessors.

Even **unbelievers** who **inquire** and discover these laws, may apply them and become **winners** in life.

On the other hand, even **believers** who do **not inquire** and discover these laws, nor apply them, may live their lives as physical and material losers.

God's plan is for His children to run this world, to possess its treasures, to monopolize its wealth, to enjoy it and to utilize it.

But He has decreed laws. **Anyone** who will discover them will reap their rich harvest, whether that person is a believer or an unbeliever.

Jesus said: *He makes the sun to rise on the evil and on the good, and sends rain on the just and on the unjust.* Mat.5:45

The Principle of Winning

A **believer** who is undisciplined and slothful in business principles, will not prosper regardless of "spirituality." He or she may pray for a material miracle, but will end up with nothing.

On the other hand, an **unbeliever**, who is astute, decisive and diligent in business principles, may act upon God's laws of success, and end up with an empire.

This is the same as to say that a **believer** who will not till the soil and plant the field, may seem "spiritual" and may pray for a harvest miracle, but he or she will end up in poverty. An **unbeliever** who tills the soil and plants the field, will reap a rich harvest.

God is trusting us to discover His laws of success, to discipline ourselves as His family members, and to become the material empire builders of His world.

Chapter 10

SEVEN BASICS
OF POSITIVE DESIRE

HERE ARE the steps which lead to your dynasty of desire.

1ST **The vision of a better life** motivates you to **INQUIRE** about God's ideas, reconsider religious taboos, reassess what the wealth of this earth is placed here for, who it is entrusted to, and to discover God's laws which are available to help anyone achieve whatever they desire.

2ND **You learn enough about God's abundant goodness** to dare to **ADMIRE** His good things in life.

3RD **You think about God's rich, unlimited resources** until you dare to **ASPIRE** to the good life for His glory and for humanity's good.

4TH **You look into God's law of liberty and realm of wealth** until, convinced of their value, you decide that you **REQUIRE** His good things in order for His kingdom to prevail among people.

5TH **You become decisive enough about your desire** for God's good life to **PERSPIRE**, if need be, to stake new claims and to achieve new goals in life.

6TH **You become so convinced that you are re-born into royalty and that God's best belongs to you**, that you no longer wait for it; you reach out and take what is yours; you possess it as your rightful domain and you **ACQUIRE** it.

7TH **You utilize the abundant goodness of God** that is manifested in your life to **INSPIRE**, to lift, to improve and to bless your world around you with your overflow.

These seven principles of THE POSITIVE POWER OF DESIRE are God's laws. They will work for **anyone** who is disciplined, decisive, committed and diligent enough to put them into action.

Chapter 11

WE HAVE GOD'S DREAM

WHY SHOULD unbelieving philosophers be the discoverers and publishers of the success secrets which God has decreed for this universe?

As long as believers condemn the good life and eulogize poverty, God's people will not have dominion on this earth as He has trusted us to have.

God has committed His dream to us. It is up to us to become the winners we are destined to be. His life in us will be the source and the force of our success, but it cannot be released in us until we **inquire** and **know** our rights, and put our faith into action in the material realm.

The issues of objectivity, goal-setting, decisiveness, commitment, perseverance, positive attitude, success, winning, influence and growth are almost always addressed by theologians and Bible teachers in a "spiritual" sense.

Little or no practical instruction, based on Bible principles, is given in church circles to help believers to achieve material success.

God's Headquarters at Our House

Those enterprises are considered carnal and threatening to "spiritual" growth.

So-called Bible believers often concentrate on their "spiritual" warfare, and tend to brand any application of practical laws for material success as "humanism."

When Jesus Christ becomes Lord in any life, that man or that woman is then a member of God's family, of divine royalty, of God's kingdom or domain, and **His seat of authority and action is then headquartered in that person.**

When God and a human person are reunited, it is not for the purpose of just sitting and communing together about **spiritual** blessings.

God has restored us to the position for which He originally created Adam and Eve. We are *justified by faith in Jesus Christ.*Rom.5:1 It is as though we had never sinned. Now we are His ambassadors. Now we are to *subdue and replenish the earth.* We are to *have dominion over it.*Gen.1:28

Succeeding with God

To fulfill God's dream, God's believing people are to control the wealth which He has entrusted to them.

We can do it if we will stop "spiritualizing" the laws of success and stop our superstitious branding of common sense laws as "humanism."

Let believers build the great enterprises of this world.

Let believers become the winning politicians who govern the nations.

Let believers be the world's great thinkers.

Let believers discover, develop and disseminate the success laws for achievement.

Let believers be the reputed success teachers for business and industry.

Let believers control the wealth of this world.

Let believers own and run the airlines, the shipping companies, and the freight monopolies of this world.

Let believers become the business magnates of this world.

Let believers become the oil barons and the industrial giants of this century.

Let believers become the artists and the poets, the judges and the lawyers, the governors and the mayors of society.

WE HAVE GOD'S DREAM

Let believers utilize the wealth
created by our Father and
entrusted to our control, to
teach, publish and proclaim
the gospel of Jesus Christ
to all of our world.

Chapter 12

SUCCESS IS GOD'S IDEA

W HY SHOULD Napoleon Hill or Dale Carnegie or Clement Stone or Ralph Waldo Emerson or Orison Swett Marden or James Allen or any of the scores of other renowned and capable writers be the only great inquirers, discoverers and disseminators of the principles of success?

Every true success principle about which they have written is rooted in the teachings of great Bible characters such as Moses, Abraham, Joshua, Ezra, Nehemiah, David, Solomon, Jesus Christ our Lord, the apostle Paul, James, John and others.

The philosophers and sages of the past were not exposed to the profusion of positive teaching about faith in God that people hear today. The negative theology of a medieval ecclesiastical hierarchy so infected their mentality that there was no motivation for them to relate success principles to their true Bible source in God.

Yet those great philosophical minds inquired diligently after the principles of success, and as the industrialized world began to blossom in

Western civilization, they set themselves to discover and to publish the principles of success laws
for society.

Wary of the theological condemnation of positive thinking and of human development, they
dared not mention God lest their writings be stig-
matized.

Progressiveness was assumed by religious circles to be the potentially dangerous influence of
atheistic philosophers.

These writers couched their references to God
in strange terms like "Infinite Intelligence," "The
Master Mind" or "The Cosmic Force." Yet, despite
their lack of exposure to positive faith teaching
from the Bible, and despite the prejudices they
confronted, they discovered the essence of principles which have brought success to millions, and
they shared their secrets using the terms with
which they were most familiar.

Instead of naively accusing their works as the
devil's formula of "humanism," let believers **inquire** after these laws, derive the good which is
already sought out, compiled, organized, outlined
and published (omitting or correcting what is un-
scriptural), **and let them hook these success principles to God's Bible formula and teach them and
publish them so that believers in God can become the business and industrial giants in our
world.**

God's Wealth Is for Everyone

God never intended that anyone should go through life imprisoned in the jail of their own patriarchal superstitions. **He opens the door of success to every believer who will dare to step out and go after the good life.**

No one in God's family was ever destined to exist in the prison of sickness or of fear, of ignorance or of poverty, of loneliness or of mediocrity.

God's abundant goodness belongs to the **many** — and it will be enjoyed and utilized by the **many** when the **many** discipline themselves, become decisive, bold, adventurous, believing, daring, risking and determined. It belongs to the **many** who dare to set high goals, apply success principles, determine to persevere, never give up, and possess and rule their share of the material world which God has entrusted to them.

SECTION II

ADMIRE

WHAT IS WRONG with wanting more? Why settle for just a piece of the sky? Where is it written that you dare not find the meaning of the new morning you see?

Why can your eyes see so far if you are designed for a dingy corner?

Why is the sky so vast if you are not meant to reach for the stars?

Why is the rainbow so glorious if you are not meant to look up?

If you **admire** the good life, are you guilty of covetousness? Should you be condemned for pride?

You are born to ADMIRE what is beautiful, good and productive. God wants you to soar on a scale which religious prejudice would forbid you to even dream about.

Chapter 13

A NEW LOOK–
A BETTER LIFE

YOU HAVE STOPPED, looked and listened enough to dare to **INQUIRE** about the good life, sorting out the difference between guilt and God, between tradition and truth, between condemnation and common sense.

Your **inquiry** has opened the door to beautiful new horizons. You have dared to **ADMIRE** them. You have raised the blinds, broken off the shackles and knocked down the walls which had restrained you.

In Barbara Streisand's powerful film, YENTL, the bright young lady grows up under her rabbi father's religious dominance. She, as a female, is forbidden an education, prohibited from reading rabbinical books, restrained from knowledge, banned from inquiry and predestined to a lifetime of female inferiority and servitude.

Her insatiable hunger for knowledge, and her determined inquisitiveness drove her to break sacred rules, to steal into her father's library **and dare to read the Talmud.** Finally she disguised herself as a male in order to pursue talmudic studies at a yeshiva—the sacred domain of "holy" males, the forbidden terrain for "lowly" females.

But she is finally alienated from her people and journeys off into the distance with a boatload of seemingly displaced nonpersons in search of a land that is free of religious bigotry.

Her sin? **She dared to INQUIRE** beyond pharisaical limits, **and she dared to ADMIRE** what parochial bigots prohibited females to even dream about. **She had the daring idea that God must be as good to women as He is to men.**

You Have a Voice! You Have a Choice!

As Yentl struggles with her free spirit and grapples with religious prejudice, she expresses her desperate search in some terrific songs.

She asks: **Where is it written that I cannot be the person I am meant to be?**

Describing the narrow views religion has permitted her to glimpse, she realized that she had only been allowed to see **a piece of sky.** Now she had **stepped outside and looked around, having never dreamed the sky was so wide or so high.**

Yentl is born into a new world by her new knowledge. **She has a voice now. She has a choice now.**

Then some of her masterpiece lines are:

What is wrong with wanting more? Why settle for just a piece of the sky?

Greater Possibility

Though scandalized by religious repression, she can now **walk through the forests of the trees of knowledge and listen to the lessons of the leaves.**

She sings about **certain things which once you have, no wind can blow away, no tide can turn away, no fire can burn away, no time can wear away.**

Her closing songs become intense prayers of praise and of affirmation by the new Yentl who has been born because she dared to INQUIRE, then to ADMIRE the wonder of knowledge.

See Yourself! Free Yourself! Be Yourself!

She feels that she is **wrapped in a robe of light, clothed in God's glory.** Exuberantly, she asks, **Why is a bird given wings, if not to fly? Why have eyes to see and not see? Or arms to reach and not reach? Or a mind unless you're meant to question why? Or why have thirst if not to drink?**

She asks again, **Where is it written that I dare not find the meaning of the new morning that I see?**

Yentl is free. She reflects on the years when she **only wanted the shadows; but shadows can never satisfy her again.**

She remembers when **she had run from the sunlight, afraid that she had seen too much. She had held in her feelings and closed every door. But she would not close them anymore.**

Now something tells her **to SEE herself, to FREE herself, to BE herself** at last. Too long **the curtains had been drawn.** Now she could **welcome the dawn. She could not keep the voice inside her quiet any longer.** No matter what happened, **it could never be the same anymore.** She promised herself **it would NEVER be the same anymore.**

The entire, moving story, dramatizes the glorious exuberance of a human person who has at last been able to extricate herself from the demoralizing shadows of repressive dogmatism and prejudice.

Better Than Your Dreams

Now the taboos are being exposed for **you** too. You are daring to step out under the vast open sky of God's abundance.

The trees are taller, the forests are richer, the mountains are higher, the sky is bigger than you ever dreamed.

And your good judgment tells you that your Father created it all for **you.**

Reflecting on your past, limited by religious forebodings and forewarnings of damnation and doom if you dared to **admire what you desire,** you are asking:

** **Why can my eyes** see so far if I am designed for a dingy corner?

** **Why do the birds** sing, why does the breeze blow, if I am not designed to enjoy the music and to inhale the wind?

** **Why is the earth** so productive if I am not meant to harvest all I can seed?

** **Why is the sky** so vast if I am not meant to reach for the stars?

** **Why are the roses** so fragrant if I am not meant to savor their aroma?

** **Why is the rainbow** so glorious if I am not meant to look up?

Chapter 14

CAPACITY FOR ACHIEVEMENT

THE NEGATIVE SIDE of religion condemns and indicts people for almost everything that is materially pleasurable and physically enjoyable.

There are scores of Bible verses which warn about *the lust of the flesh, the lust of the eyes and the pride of life.*[1Jn.2:16]

But religion has majored on those scriptures so much that any desire for material prosperity has been incriminated. Believers dare not **inquire** after or **admire** the abundant wealth God has created for His family lest they be guilty of covetousness and condemned for pride.

But unless the taboos of material blessings are rejected, believers will never exercise the positive faith necessary to a successful enterprise for the good of God, of yourself and of people.

Why all the beauty on earth, if not for us?

Why all the wealth, if not for believers?

Why all the potential for achievement, and why all the workable laws of success if not for God's people?

Why all the good things in life, if not for His family?

You Are Not Limited

The reason this book is in your hands is because God wants you to know that it is not wrong to desire progress and better living.

Hooked up with God, there is no limit to your source for achievement.

Since the day God created Adam and Eve in an environment of abundance, happiness, health and fulfillment, He has never changed His mind about people.

You have the miraculous capacity that no other creature has — to **think** and **plan**, to **ponder** and **imagine**, to **believe** and **achieve**, to **acquire** what you **desire**.

With your tie to desire and your eye to acquire, you have...

The **principle** of inspiration,
The **basis** for enthusiasm,
The **trigger** for action,
The **stimulus** for endurance,
The **motive** for achievement,
The **inducement** for improvement.

God says: *Listen to me and you will have a long, good life. Carry out my instructions, for they will lead you to real living.*Prov.4:10,13LB

He is saying, "Step outside under My big skies. Lift up your eyes. Take a look. It is beautiful. Love it. **Admire** it. I made it all for **you**. It is **your** domain. If you **admire** it, you can **acquire** it."

Jesus said: *Whatever things you desire, when you pray, believe that you receive them, and you will have them.*Mk.11:24

But you must **inquire** about them and **admire** the things you **desire**, in order to **acquire** them.

Be Aware—Never Despair

When I researched what theologians have written on this subject, I found volumes which condemned, impugned and indicted the carnality of desire.

But I found that encouragement for believers to aim for the top in material success was scarce.

I know that to desire riches or wealth or any other thing because of greed, jealousy, avarice or lust is both self-destructive and counter-productive.

I know about Ahab's greed for Naboth's vineyard and how he was so consumed that he died there.

I know about Joseph's brothers selling him because of greed and jealousy, and of the humiliating result of their deed.

I know about David's lust for Bathsheba that caused him to sin before God, and the deep remorse that consumed him.

I know about the rich man who heaped his wealth to consume it in riotous living and how his soul was required of him.

I know about Judas and his self-destruction over greed and lust for a measly thirty pieces of silver.

I know many reasons to warn against evil desire. But I believe that Christian writings should emphasize encouragement for believers to desire the good things God has created on this planet for them.

Because of sermonizers who stress the negative side of desire, believers give up and back off, because they are programmed for guilt. Satan, the accuser, [Rev.12:10] makes them believe that their desire for success is motivated wrongly. That is his device to keep material wealth out of the hands of God's people.

Satan does not care how much *spiritual* wealth we possess, so long as we do not have the *material* means to share God's blessings with human persons.

Desire God's Best

One of the cardinal doctrines of Hinduism is to suppress all desire for any blessing, or status, or happiness, or success in life. It teaches that we are the product of fate; that whatever state we are in, we are to accept it with resignation.

Buddha taught that human persons could achieve a level of mental control where all desires in life would be neutralized and that the very root of desire would die. He called this "Nirvana" or DESIRELESSNESS.

But the very yearning for the state of desirelessness is in itself desire. In fact, it is so intense that one may spend a lifetime struggling in desperate mental search of achieving this paradise of neutrality. It is like trying to cure a headache by getting rid of the head.

We are created with the emotional capacity to ADMIRE what is beautiful, good and productive.

God wants those healthy emotions in you **freed** so you can soar to new levels and bless your world on a scale which religious prejudice would forbid you to even dream about.

Chapter 15

THE MASTER
SUCCESS TEACHER

ANGELS ANNOUNCED Christ's coming by saying, *We have glad tidings of great joy for ALL people. Behold a Savior is born.*Lu.2:10-11

A Savior from what?

From the judgment of our sins? Surely. But also from the curse of deterioration, self-deprecation and insignificance. From sickness and disease, from poverty and failure, from mediocrity and humiliation, from disobedience and death.

Jesus came as a Savior from the negativism of religion that condemns, demoralizes, threatens and negates human personhood.

Religion has always been cruel, esteeming laws as being more sacred than lives.

Jesus healed a poor man with a withered hand. The religious crowd yelled: It's the wrong day. Leave his hand crippled. Respect the Sabbath.Mk.3:1-6

They cared more for their law than for a poor man's crippled hand.

Jesus raised a man from the dead who had been in his tomb for four days. The religious crowd never glorified God but recoiled and took counsel to kill Jesus, lest the people follow Him.[Jn.11:45]

They were so preoccupied about their control over people's minds that even the restoring of life to a man who had been dead for four days never affected their dogmatism. They preferred to ignore the miracle and to kill Jesus rather than to risk losing their manipulative influence over the people.

They brought a woman to Jesus who had been taken in the act of adultery. The religious crowd wanted to stone her to death for breaking the law.

Jesus treated her like a lady and restored her self-esteem by forgiving her.[Jn.8:4-11]

Jesus encountered a naked maniac. The religious crowd had no interest in him, but left him to his torment and hoped he would die.

Jesus restored his mind and gave him a position of honor. He sent him to the ten towns of the Decapolis as His personal representative.[Mk.5:1-20] What an honor!

Jesus met an unclean leper. The religious crowd left him to his fate. But Jesus cleansed him so that he could have honor and dignity as a respected citizen again.[Mk.1:40-45]

Jesus came to this world to show people what God is like. He said, *If you have seen me, you have seen the Father.*[Jn.14:9] *I am in the Father and the Father is in me.*[Jn.14:11]

Jesus was good. He was non-judgmental. He was happy. He had everything He ever needed. Nature was at His command. He was powerful. He lifted, blessed, helped, healed and loved people.

He showed us the kind of life the Father wants us to enjoy.

Wonders of the Miracle Worker

He said, *ALL THINGS whatever you desire,*[Mk.11:24] you can have them.

He said, *With God, ALL THINGS are possible.*[Mk.10:27]

He said, *Nothing will be impossible for you.*[Mat.17:20]

He found a fisherman and made him a leader.

He transformed a demon-possessed, abused woman into a lady and one of His most productive followers.

He lifted a naked maniac from living torment and shame into an effective representative for Him.

He changed a cheating tax-collector into a gentleman of respect.

He took ugly things and made them beautiful.

He replaced terminal disease with radiant health.

He superseded the laws of justice and crowned them with the wonders of mercy.

He stopped death in its tracks and transcended it with a new infusion of life.

He saw limitless possibilities everywhere.

Ordinary people became extraordinary when they discovered Him.

He helped people discover the **good** life.

He taught only the **Good** News.

He influenced people who were diseased by guilt, plagued by defeat, overwhelmed by problems and frustrated by prejudice to stand up tall and proud and to discover that God believes in them and wills His best for them in happiness, health, success and self-esteem.

Chapter 16

BELIEVERS WITH POSITIVE DESIRE

WHEN GOD FINISHED creating this world, He was so pleased that **He took time out to look over what He had made for the people He had created in His image.**

And God saw [admired] *every thing that he had made, and behold, IT WAS VERY GOOD.*Gen.1:31

Dare we allow pious bigotry to label as bad what God admired as **good**?

God Admires You

Once you set your eyes on God's better lifestyle, you will not cower and retreat when the going is rough. You will transform each problem into an opportunity for growth. You will dream greater dreams than ever and with God's help, you will make those dreams come true.

If your hopes are dashed by opposition, you will not cringe in fear of judgment, but you will pick up the pieces, learn by your mistakes, profit by learning your enemy's strategy and go right back after the **best**, setting your aims higher every round.

The Bible will vibrate with new meaning.

They that seek the Lord shall **not want any good thing.**Psa.34:10

You **admire** His **good things.** You set your aim to go for them. You **acquire them.**

The Lord is your shepherd, you **shall not want.**Psa.23:1

The Lord your God brings you into a good land of brooks and fountains and springs, of wheat and barley and vines and fig trees and pomegranates, of olive oil and honey; a land where you shall eat bread without scarceness and you shall **not lack anything.**Deut.8:7-9

Second Thoughts—New Thoughts

The great leader, Nehemiah, reminded the people about how God had taken care of them throughout their historic wilderness journey. Nehemiah did this at a time when the people had allowed opposition to beat them down. Most of them had decided to content themselves with their oppressed lot.

Nehemiah provoked them to **inquire** about God's blessings. He motivated them to **admire** God's lifestyle so much that they would throw off their bondage and go after God's best with a new attitude of **winning.**

He prayed to God and said:

Forty years you sustained them in the wilderness so that they lacked nothing; their clothes waxed not old, and their feet swelled not.

*You gave them kingdoms and nations. Their children multiplied as the stars of heaven. They possessed lands, subdued enemies, inhabited the country.*Neh.9:21-24

This challenged the people to think new about their situation and to repossess the good life.

You see, it is right for you to DESIRE good things, to INQUIRE about them and to ADMIRE them like God, who created them, does.

*He **fulfills the desires** of those who reverence and trust him.*Psa.145:19LB

Never allow religion to so exaggerate the negative side of desire that you allow yourself to stifle THE POWER OF POSITIVE DESIRE.

Believe in Positive Desire

You understand that Jesus Christ redeemed you out of the realm of your **old** nature. You refuse guilt for desiring the better life. Your desire is God's desire now. You believe in the **new** creation—the **new you** that He has made you to be.

*Your old evil desires were nailed to the cross with Christ.*Rom.6:6LB

*Those who belong to Christ have nailed their natural evil desires to his cross and crucified them there.*Gal.5:24LB

God says:

*I will give you a new heart. I will give you new and right desires. I will put a new spirit within you.*Eze.36:26LB

The Lord sent messengers and said, Tell humankind, I am coming to save you and I will bring many gifts. Isa.62:11LB

You will be called "The Holy People" and "The Lord's Redeemed," and [where you live] *shall be called "The Land of Desire" and "The City God Has Blessed.*Isa. 62:12LB

Ours is **the good land, the good life.**

Admire it! GO FOR IT! (Read my book, THE BEST OF LIFE.)

Walk Honest and Lack Nothing

Jesus' story of the prodigal son illustrated the wealth, happiness and abundance prevalent **at the father's house.** But when the discontented son abandoned the lifestyle of his father's household, *he began to be in WANT.*Lu.15:14

The apostle Paul said, *Do your own business, work with your own hands. Walk honest so that you may have **lack of nothing.***1Th.4:11-12

Those who will be succeeding ten or twenty years from now will be those who believe in THE POWER OF POSITIVE DESIRE. They believe that what

God created is **their domain**, refusing the restrictions of imposed prejudice.

They do like Abraham did when God told *him to lift up your eyes, and look northward, southward, eastward and westward; for all the land that you SEE, to you will I give it and to your seed forever.*[Gen.13:14-15]

Arise, walk through the land in the length of it and the breadth of it; for I will give it to you.[Gen.13:17]

God created man and woman for excellence, success, exhilaration, self-esteem, health, happiness and abundance in His *Good Life*. He never designed His own offspring, made *"in his own likeness and image,"* for mediocrity, insignificance, disease, poverty or guilt.

From the breathtaking grandeur of mountain peaks to the fabulous rich valleys of our planet, God placed humanity amidst a rich world of GOOD things for their usefulness, beauty and pleasure.

He said, *"Instead of shame and dishonor, you shall have a double portion of prosperity and everlasting joy, and all shall realize that you are a people God has blessed."* Isa. 61:7,9 Living Bible

"If you want a happy, GOOD LIFE, ... trust yourself to Christ your Lord." 1Pet. 3:10,15 Living Bible

"No GOOD thing will He withhold from them that walk uprightly before Him." Psalm 84:11

SECTION III

ASPIRE

YOU ARE BEYOND admiration. Deep inside you, yearning power is burning in you.

> Every compliment sets the stage
>   for another improvement.
> Every accomplishment sets the gage
>   for a higher measurement.
> Every achievement turns the page
>   for another treasure hunt.

Aspire to the good things God has created in this world. They are placed here for you—in partnership with Him. When you aspire to the good life, it is Him at work in you **aspiring** to utilize His BEST for His kingdom.

> When our desire is tuned to God's
>   aspirations,
> Then our empire can bloom with
>   His inspirations.

Chapter 17

ENERGIZED
FOR ACHIEVEMENT

WAS GOD'S original dream bad or good? Restricted or unlimited? Stingy or generous? Demoralizing or exhilarating? Discouraging or uplifting? Sickly or healthy? Demeaning or self-esteeming?

The real fire of desire is burning in you. Your **admiration** has turned to **aspiration**.

You see abundant possibilities for lifting your world, for doing good, for healing hurts, for lifting loads, for blessing the downtrodden, for meeting needs, for sharing life, for spreading hope, for enriching people, for achievement, fulfillment, happiness, objectivity, prosperity and success.

You will never again be content with only a piece of the sky. You will march amidst God's tallest trees. You will climb the highest mountains, mine the greatest treasures and sail the deepest seas. It is **your** world, **your** domain. God created it for **you**.

Never the Same Again

You are His co-worker. The emotions you feel are His emotions being reflected through you.

*It is God who is at work within you, giving you the will and the power to achieve his purpose.*Phil.2:13LB

One translation says: *God is the **energizer** within you.* The same one says: *There are varieties of things accomplished but the same God does the **energizing** in them all.*1Cor.12:6

You say, "Now I will not only be fulfilled and happy myself; I will be able to do God's work."

God is going to use all that He has created, which He declares is **good**, to bless you, then to make you a blessing.

Jesus said, *The Father that dwells with me, he will do the work.*Jn.14:10 God made the abundant good that surrounds you. He wills to use it to bless you and to bless others through you.

Denis Waitley said—among many other good lines:

It's not your talent, or the gifted birth,
It's not your bank book that proves your worth;
Just grab your dream and then believe it,
Go out and work, and you'll achieve it.

Chapter 18

POSITIVE YEARNING POWER

YOUR ADMIRING lifts you to a new level. You begin to **ASPIRE** to the good life.

Aspire, among other meanings, is to have deep yearning and noble desire or ambition, to have ardent desire for what is great and good. To aim high. To endeavor with eagerness.

You are here to **be**, to **have** and to **do** the Father's good pleasure—to embrace and then disseminate the Good News to everyone.

Aspire to Go Higher

You are hooked up with God to do **the big kingdom business of blessing all who choose to believe.** You have purpose. You have self-dignity. You experience a new birth of your own worth.

You **must** have dominion because you are in union with God. The good things God has created are no longer an **option to be admired;** they are **the top ones to be acquired.**

One writer said, your **yearning** power is more vital than your **earning** power.

Cicero said, "The thirst of desire is never fulfilled." And that is true.

I have said:

> Every compliment sets the stage
> for another improvement.

> Every accomplishment sets the gage
> for a higher measurement.

> Every achievement turns the page
> for another treasure hunt.

Do you aspire to better health, a better home or car or job, companionship, better relationships with people, a keener awareness of God, more happiness and fulfillment, more money, greater influence, a happier marriage, more love?

After you have decided what you really desire, then write it down and look at it. Begin to see yourself with it. Read your list out loud, every day.

The Will to Win

Do like Wilma Rudolph did when she was a child. Though polio paralyzed both legs, twisting her left foot inward, and burdening her with two leg braces, she never stopped dreaming that she would break out of her handicap and succeed in life.

Her whole being **aspired** to triumph over her obstacles.

Her incredible force of faith and unwavering aspiration to achieve distinction drove her to shed those braces and to force her leg nerves and muscles into action.

Astounding everyone, she taught herself to walk, made the basketball team, then became a runner and captured the hearts of fans around the world by three electrifying Olympic performances in which she brought home three gold medals — the first woman in history to ever do it. The formerly crippled girl became a living legend.

She **aspired** to achievement, and nothing could stop her. One of America's great baseball coaches is credited with saying: "Winning isn't everything, but **the will to win** is everything."

Dream Impossible Dreams

Sincerely **aspire** to the good things God has created in this world. Accept the fact that they are placed here for you — in partnership with God. When you aspire to the good life, it is God at work in you **aspiring** to utilize His BEST for His kingdom.

People who win in life concentrate on what they aspire to and ignore whatever limitations they may face.

1. **DREAM** beyond what is possible to you.

2. ASPIRE to what you dream about.

3. DRIVE for your dreams.

Burton says, "Wise people will desire no more than they can get justly, use sensibly, distribute cheerfully and leave contentedly."

While his advice is basically good, it is negative.

I would rather encourage you to set your goals high by saying:

> Be wise with God's wisdom.
>
> Acquire as much as His creative ideas in you will produce.
>
> He will inspire you to use it sensibly.
>
> You will share it in ways that glorify God and that lift people.
>
> When you die, you will leave it in channels where it will finance God's best dreams.

When you get God's viewpoint and see the abundance He created for you, you will rise and go for the good life.

Helen Keller once said, "We can do anything if we desire enough to do it, and if we stick to it!"

The good life is God's idea.

*The desire of the righteous is only good.*Prov.11:23

When God is alive in you, **you** aspire to what **He** aspires to — that aspiration is good.

Real Zest for Living

Balguy says, "When your aspirations are boundless, your labors are endless. They set you a task you can never complete and require work you can never finish. Satisfaction is always absent; happiness is always distant."

But that philosophy represses your development.

I would rather encourage your boundless aspirations because **unlimited desire** is the motivator for **unlimited faith.** It is the reason for **unceasing action** and that gives **zest for living.**

It is true that every problem you solve will only produce a bigger one, but that opens the path to greater opportunities and bigger accomplishments.

Satisfaction and happiness are not distant goals but every day realizations, when we discover that **desiring is inspiring** and that **yearning power is earning power.**

Chapter 19

WE NEED
GOD'S STUFF—NOW

HEAVEN already has **enough**.

Here on earth we need **God's stuff.**

Religion, in its many brands, invariably links penury with piety, suffering with holiness, and burdens with humility.

Emerson, the great American philosopher, says that from the time he was a lad, he wanted to write an essay that would deal with traditional theology which indoctrinates people against aspiring to material success, achievement, and prosperity.

In his inimitable way he said that real life, as people live it, "is **ahead of theology** and that **people know more than the preacher."**

Then he explained how a preacher talked about life and the Last Judgment as though every issue would have to await its outcome. By this doctrine the preacher ignored the fact that you reap what you sow and get what you strive for, **here in this life as well as in the next.**

Mr. Emerson was shocked at the preacher's doctrine for he emphasized that **only the wicked should be successful in this world** and that good people should prove their humility and piety by living lives of misery.

But then the preacher extolled the fact that God would balance the scales at the great Judgment Day. **Then,** and not before, the wicked would get their **deserved misery** and the righteous would **inherit riches.**

But it was all **spiritualized.** There was nothing for the righteous **here and now** in this material world.

Plenty in Earth— Plenty in Heaven

In other words, Mr. Emerson said, the preacher applauded riches for the righteous—**in heaven,** but deplored the thought of material prosperity for them **here and now.**

He said, in essence, the preacher is teaching his parishioners to say: **"In this material world,** we will submit and suppress our desires and live like paupers, while the wicked revel in their sinful material luxury.

"But once we get to heaven, we will no longer cower in submission, suppression and deprivation. We shall stand up and revel in all of the riches that the wicked have here on earth."

In other words, "It is a sin to be rich here and now. **We who are pious shall not sin now, but we shall sin in heaven;** we would like to sin now, but we shall get our revenge later."

To young Emerson, this was nonsense. Though he understood little about the Bible, it seemed illogical to him that the **wicked should prosper** and that the **righteous should be poor.** Why not the reverse?

The Good News is just the reverse!

Jesus taught: *Thy will be done in earth, as it is in heaven.* Mat.6:10

For what purposes will the righteous need silver and gold in heaven?

Here on earth is where the wealth God created can be put to work for the good.

God does not need the treasures He placed on this earth. He has plenty in heaven.

One of the greatest sins might be to refuse to discipline ourselves, apply our talents and achieve material success — here and now.

The Bible teaches that God rewards faith **now,** as well as in heaven.

Faith is your **aspiration** turned Godward.

Let your desire soar to the level of God's desires for you.

Miraculous changes will begin to take place in your life when you do.

Chapter 20

ASPIRE TO YOUR DOMAIN

GOD WANTS YOU to realize that within you is the possibility to shed the cloak of failure, to escape the negative syndrome of discouragement, to break with the demoralizing dogmas of defeat, to get out of the boredom of conformity and to go for life at its best.

Aspire to more than the average person settles for. A common characteristic of all winners is, **they deeply aspire to win.**

The force of eager aspiration in you has a miraculous way of releasing powerful energy, creativity and an almost supernatural pull toward what you yearn for.

One of the most vital facts you will discover is that God wants you to have good things — the best in life, but He must wait until you **aspire to have them, and go for them** before He can give them to you.

When a blind man cried out to Jesus, He stopped and asked him, "What do you **want** me to do for you?" He **wanted** his sight, and he received it.

Dreams Do Come True

Until we have a dream, we can never know what it is to have a dream come true.

The pious religionist crucifies our wants by vilifying our desires, which is like lopping off our feet because we want shoes.

The Bible says that *by God's mighty power at work within us, he is able to do far more than we would* **dare** *to* **ask** *or even* **dream** *of — infinitely beyond our highest* **prayers, desires, thoughts** *or* **hopes.**[Eph.3:20LB]

Aspire to all that God has created.

Let go of all religious taboos regarding material blessings and happiness.

You deserve the BEST in life. That is why God created it and put you here in the middle of it. **It is your domain.**

Read my book, THE MESSAGE THAT WORKS, and discover God's total supply for your total lifestyle.

People who accuse the prosperous and condemn the affluent often hoard and conceal their miserly stocks for their own futures, never enjoying the pleasure of God's material blessing in the now, and certainly never lifting others.

This world and its wealth is **our domain.**

But we can never possess this pearl of great price until we understand its value and ASPIRE to possess it for our good, for the blessing of other people around us and for the glory of God.

We Are the Masters

God never gave us a world already developed and accomplished.

He entrusted us with the seed **to plant,** the soil **to cultivate,** the oceans **to sail,** the mountains **to scale,** the deserts **to conquer,** the rivers **to harness,** the minerals **to mine,** the forests **to utilize,** plus a brain and a spirit **to receive His creative ideas** for doing these things.

With Him at work in us, we can **be,** and **have,** and **do** anything He puts into our spirit and mind to do. We are to be the masters of this world.

Never forget what Jesus said, *Ask, seek, knock. Everyone that asks receives.*[Mat.7:7-8]

How simple! If you really **want** it, if you earnestly **aspire** to it enough to ask, to seek and to knock, **you will get it**.

Jesus said to a woman who intensely wanted Him to heal her daughter — and who would not give up: *Be it as you desire.*[Mat.15:28] And the girl was healed.

*When you delight in God, he gives you the **desires** of your heart. You will **inherit** the earth. God will exalt you to **inherit** the land.*[Psa.37:4,9,34]

There is **plenty** of everything for you, if you are convinced of **your** value and really **aspire** to the BEST in life.

Chapter 21

EMPIRE OF DESIRE

THE MEASURE of what you allow God to **be,** to **do,** or **have** in and through you, depends upon **the intensity of your aspiration** to **be** or **do** or **have** His best for **you,** for **Him** and for **others.**

David said, *My heart and my flesh cries out for the living God.*Psa.84:2

*My soul thirsts for God, my flesh longs for him.*Psa.63:1

Our spirits **yearn** for God, for peace, for tranquility, for meaning and for achievement.

Our flesh **aspires** to the physical and material provisions God has created for us — water, food, air, comforts, success, wealth, abundance, health, happiness and fulfillment.

If those aspirations are suppressed and not allowed to motivate us, we will die in nothingness and emptiness, without purpose or significance.

One writer said, "To really **aspire** after the good life means to really **pray** for it."

You will **pray** for it and **believe** for it when you **know** about it.

Lifting Power

As long as you demean what God has paid so much to redeem, as long as you put down what cost God so much to lift up and as long as you condemn what God paid so dearly to forgive, you will be repressed by religion and continue to bow under the burdens of bigotry.

Jesus Christ came to give you self-esteem.

He never, ever put anyone down—except religious people who used their religion to put people down. He is a lifter of people, a healer, a restorer.

He wants to restore your faith in life, if circumstances have broken your will.

If you are poor, He wants to give you hope and faith that good things in life are for you.

If you have been blind to your value, to your potential or to the possibilities around you, Jesus Christ wants to open your eyes to see a dozen solutions to problems you thought were impossible to solve.

Your ears may have been stopped and you missed the answers in life. The Lord will miraculously open them and you will hear what counts for life's best.

You may have been demoralized until you withdrew in failure and humiliation. Jesus will stand up inside of you and cause you to walk tall in life, and succeed where you failed before.

Dare and Do

M. Henry warns: "If our wishes are not subject to God's providence, then our pursuits will not be restrained by His precepts."

But I prefer to state this principle in a positive way:

> *When our desire is tuned*
> *to God's aspirations,*

> *Then our empire can bloom*
> *with His inspiration.*

Jesus said: *Blessed are the ones who* **hunger** *and* **thirst, they shall be filled.**Mat.5:6

He fills the **hungry** *with* **good things.**Lu.1:53LB

The apostle Peter asked: *Do you* really **aspire** *to more of God's kindness? Learn to know him better and as you do, He will give you everything you need for living a truly good life.*2Pet.1:2-3LB

God's aspirations become yours as you discover Him at work in you.

It is God who works in you, inspiring both the **will** [the desire, the yearning, the aspiration, the Yes. I want to" *and the* **deed** [the ability to put desires into action], *for His own chosen purpose.*Phil.2:13NEB

Origin of Desire

God actually **puts His desires for good into your heart** when you have His view of life, and when you practice awareness of Him at work in you.

In 2 Chronicles 30:12 (LB) *the people felt a **strong, God-given desire*** for His way and for His best.

In Ezekiel 1:5 (LB) *God gave a **great desire** to the leaders.* They wanted to get back on the right path and build their lives God's way.

In Nehemiah 2:17-18 (LB) the people were re-minded of the tragedy of their city in ruins. Ne-hemiah said, *Let's rebuild the wall and rid ourselves of disgrace! Then he told them about the desire God had put in his heart and the plan. The people replied at once, "Good! Let's rebuild." And the work began.*

You see, when you **aspire** to good, it is God **as-piring** through you. **Your desire is God's desire.**

Health, happiness, success and fulfillment are **God's ideas.** He offers them, and their tremen-dous benefits to you. But He wants you to desire them.

Seek [aspire to] *good that you may live.*Amos5:14

God says:

*I love them that love me; and those that **seek** me early shall find me.*Prov.8:17

*Unending riches, honor, justice and righteousness are mine to distribute. My gifts are better than the purest gold or sterling silver. Those who love and follow me are indeed wealthy. I fill their treasuries.*Prov.8:18,21LB

Jesus asked some blind men:

*What do you **want** me to do for you? They said, **We want to see.** And he was moved with compassion, touched their eyes and instantly they could see, and followed him.*Mat.20:32-34LB

David said:

*Happy are those who are strong in the Lord, and who **want** above all else to follow his steps.*Psa.84:5LB

Inside of the new liberated **you,** there is a burning yearning to move out into God's limitless **empire of desire** and to make it yours.

You are ready for the next level of achievement where your whole person will actually **assume a positive resolve to get God's best,** because you have His life in perspective.

"**W**e never weary of seeing the MULTITUDES receive Christ, experience His love, and praise Him with new joy and hope. In nearly 90 nations, we have personally witnessed this wonder. It is marvelous; it never gets old. This is the MINISTRY OF JESUS to the multitudes, ONE person at a time."

—T.L. Osborn

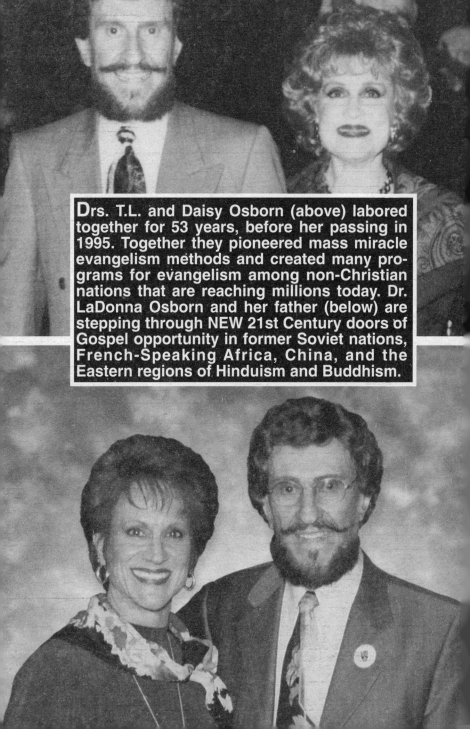

Drs. T.L. and Daisy Osborn (above) labored together for 53 years, before her passing in 1995. Together they pioneered mass miracle evangelism methods and created many programs for evangelism among non-Christian nations that are reaching millions today. Dr. LaDonna Osborn and her father (below) are stepping through NEW 21st Century doors of Gospel opportunity in former Soviet nations, French-Speaking Africa, China, and the Eastern regions of Hinduism and Buddhism.

JESUS CHRIST offers God's BEST – faith, hope, love and life to all who believe in Him, as depicted in this masterpiece painting by Gustave Doré (1832-1883).

The Osborns, ministers to millions world-wide, believe that God's abundant goodness was created for, and is the domain of all who believe and trust in His love. The positive power of desire for what *He wants,* releases His power to give you what *you want.*

Dr. Osborn teaches that God's will for you is GOOD. You can discover how He wants you to triumph over every negative situation.

Dr. T.L. Osborn and daughter, Dr. LaDonna – Vice President and CEO of the Osborn World Ministries – are involved in seminars, mass crusades and Church growth activities around the world, often on two fronts at the same time. When possible, they minister together in Gospel campaigns like this one in Central Africa. Believing that *"the Gospel is the power of God for salvation to everyone who believes,"* their life-mission is sharing Christ, His Good News and love globally, which they consider to be the ministry nearest the heart of God.

In crusades around the world, Dr. T.L. Osborn and Dr. LaDonna Osborn share God's plan for abundance with millions.

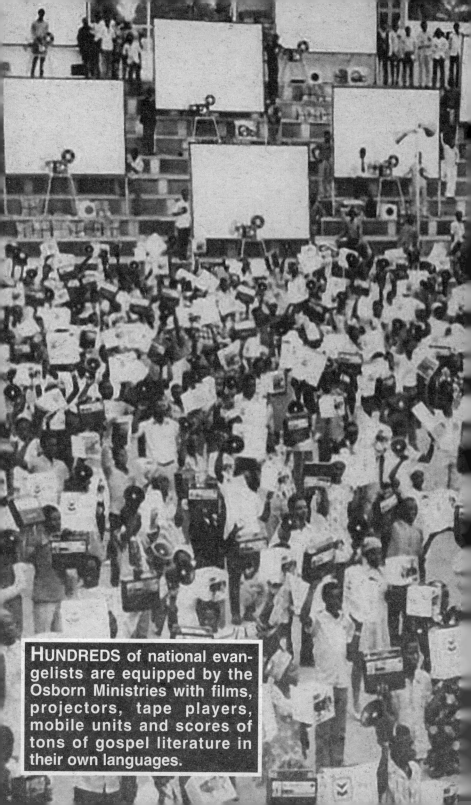

HUNDREDS of national evangelists are equipped by the Osborn Ministries with films, projectors, tape players, mobile units and scores of tons of gospel literature in their own languages.

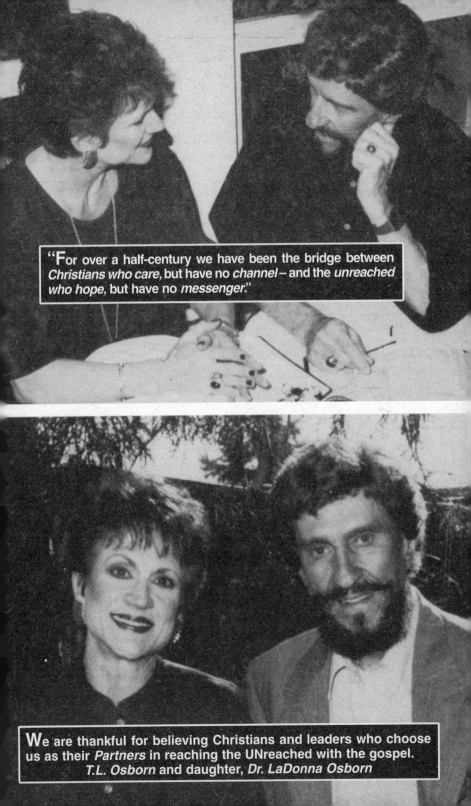

"For over a half-century we have been the bridge between *Christians who care*, but have no *channel* – and the *unreached who hope*, but have no *messenger*."

We are thankful for believing Christians and leaders who choose us as their *Partners* in reaching the UNreached with the gospel. *T.L. Osborn* and daughter, *Dr. LaDonna Osborn*

T.L. AND LADONNA OSBORN *MASS-MIRACLE CRUSADES* WORLDWIDE

The Osborns *Mass Crusades* have brought new faith, hope and love to millions of people in nearly 90 nations. They consistently go out in public parks, stadiums and open fields to proclaim the gospel, where all peoples of all faiths may attend and see, for themselves, the gospel confirmed by signs and miracles, wrought by Christ's power today.

S. PACIFIC — Surabaya, Indonesia

EUROPE – The Hague, Holland

AFRICA – Uyo, Nigeria

S. AMERICA – Bogota, Colombia

ASIA – Hyderabad, India

Drs. T.L. and LaDonna Osborn are on-the-go as a father-daughter GOSPEL TEAM. Often on two fronts at the same time, they are consistent proclaimers of GOOD NEWS and joy-filled ambassadors of Christ among people globally.

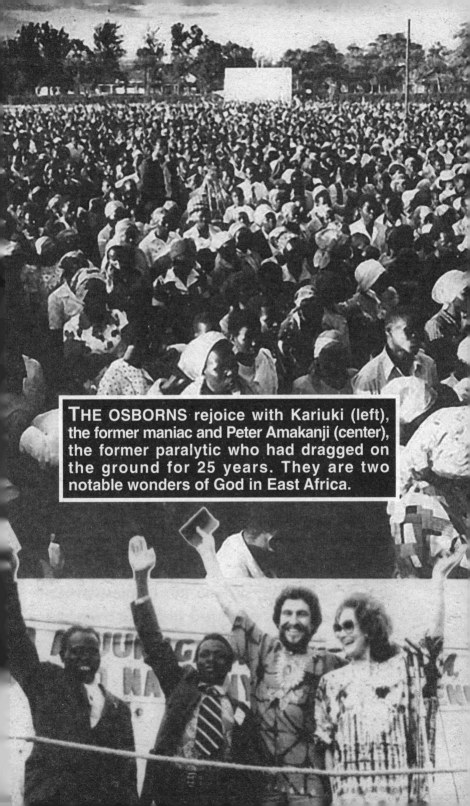

THE OSBORNS rejoice with Kariuki (left), the former maniac and Peter Amakanji (center), the former paralytic who had dragged on the ground for 25 years. They are two notable wonders of God in East Africa.

Osborn Mass Evangelism Crusades

AFRICA

S. AMERICA

INDONESIA

CARIBBEAN

PHILIPPINES

Over 100 gospel vans, equipped with Evangelism Tools, have been provided for national church organizations worldwide, by the Osborn Ministries, to facilitate them in reaching their nations with the gospel message of Jesus Christ.

OSBORN CRUSADE –
Bogota

OSBORN CRUSADE –
Accra

OSBORN CRUSADE –
S. AMERICA

OSBORN CRUSA
Nigeria

Hundreds of tape players, and thousands of the Osborns' gos

The Osborns' books and tracts are published in 132 languages (their docu-miracle crusade films, videos, and audio cassettes in 67 languages). These are scattered throughout the world, and are among the most effective Tools for Evangelism known, communicating the gospel to millions of people.

OSBORN CRUSADE –

OSBORN CRUSADE – Kinshasa

OSBORN CRUSADE – Africa

OSBORN CRUSADE – Calabar

...settes, in 67 languages, witness to millions of souls worldwide.

It is reported that the Osborns may have witnessed more miracles of physical healing than any other family. MIRACLE answers to PRAYER are not accidents or occasional phenomena. They are a result of PRAYERS that work with God's character and His provision.

Everywhere the Osborns minister – announcing and applying Christ's LOVE-message to people – miracles of physical healing occur. Why? Because God loves people and He yearns to demonstrate that reality to them. T.L. and LaDonna Osborn know how to cooperate with God's great love-plan for people.

"**A**s we stand before the MULTITUDES of needy people, our gaze is fixed on the Person of Jesus Christ. It is HIS LIFE that is expressed through us. His ministry continues through us. His words are what we declare. His love is our motivation. His passion is our mission. We are His ambassadors."
–LaDonna Osborn

SECTION IV

REQUIRE

❀

It IS YOUR trust in God's plan and in His abundant provisions that causes you to rise up, to resist limitations and to say **I REQUIRE HIS BEST so that I CAN BE HIS BEST.**

That is faith-power at work in you.

From today, say, **"No person or demon or religion or system shall restrict and restrain me, condemn and confuse me, judge and abuse me, or manipulate and maneuver me."**

Resolve that **you** shall never be frozen in unfulfillment.

Only when **you REQUIRE God's best,** can He produce His dream in and through you. **The good life is His IDEA for YOU.**

Chapter 22

REQUIRING GOD'S BEST

THE POWER OF POSITIVE DESIRE is working in you.

There is **a rich domain** to be possessed by those who believe in God. But that kingdom can only be inherited when the driving power of **desire** presses you beyond stargazing and wishful thinking.

Energy is wasted unless it is directed and focused.

There comes a time when you have dreamed enough over the sketches, plans and blueprints of your house. A decision must be made. A contract must be signed. Money must be laid on the line. A commitment must be made. The plunge must be taken. You must dare to risk everything, then GO FOR IT.

As Jesus told the fishermen, *Launch out into the deep.*Lu.5:4 It is time for you to decide: **I must have God's BEST. I REQUIRE it.** It is right and it is good.

You Deserve What You Require

Something inside you is saying, **"From today, no person or demon or religion or system is going to restrict and restrain me, condemn and confuse me, judge and abuse me, or manipulate and maneuver me."**

You are saying:

I **deserve** God's best because
He created it for me.

I **deserve** good news because
He sends it to me.

I **deserve** total happiness because
He fashioned me.

I **deserve** exhilarating health because
He is in me.

I **deserve** unlimited prosperity because
His goodness is all around me.

I **deserve** genuine love because
He forgave me.

I **deserve** a positive uplift because
He inspires me.

Only Good Things for You

You are beginning to touch and experience the exhilarating life that God created for you.

You are made for **life** and
not for death.

You are made for **health** and
not disease.

You are made for **success** and
  not for failure.

You are made for **faith** and
  not for confusion.

You are made for **love** and
  not for fear.

You are discovering that God wants **your life** to represent all of the good that He **is** and that He has created.

You have done what Jesus said to do:

You have sought first **the kingdom
of God.** You have discovered that
God's plan was to set up His love headquarters at your house.

You have sought **your right standing
in this kingdom.** You have discovered
that you and God are co-workers in
His powerful love-plan.

You have accepted His promise that
*all of these good things shall be added
to you.*^Mat.6:33

You have learned to see yourself like God sees you.

You have discovered that you are God's life at work in the **now.**

You have discovered the wonder of His grace.

You have learned to affirm:

I am part of God's plan.
I am vital to His dream.

I am an instrument in His kingdom.
I am a member of His family.

I am the proof of God's love.
I am the evidence of His life.
I am the form of His body.
I am the temple of His Spirit.

I am the expression of God's faith.
I am the fruit of His life.
I am the action of His plan.
I am the example of His seed.

Your entire outlook on life is different.

You declare:

God made me.
God believes in me.
God loves me.
God paid for me.
God never gave up on me.
God gave His Son for me.
God redeemed me.
God values me.

You are breathing fresh air. You are hearing new music. A new song is born in you.

Chapter 23

YOU ARE A MASTERPIECE

LIBERATED from religious negativism, you have made your decision.

You REQUIRE all that God has designed for you, because you have committed yourself to His loving power and to His lifting program.

Michelangelo started sculpturing at least 44 great statues in solid marble, but he only finished 14 of them. The enormous statue of David in Florence, Italy, the Pieta in Rome's basilica, and his monumental Moses are examples of his masterpieces.

Just think: At least 30 great works of art were left unfinished. Fortunately, the huge chunks of partially sculptured marble are preserved in an Italian museum. Some show only a hand or a leg or an elbow and shoulder or a foot with toes. The rest of the artist's ideas remain frozen in solid marble, locked up forever, never to be formed into his great dreams.

What about God's dream for **you?**

Resolve that **you** shall never remain frozen in unfulfillment. The material in you is the best.

The Master Sculptor has touched you with His miracle power, and is designing you to reveal Himself through.

Hidden Possibilities

The greatest tragedy in life is for people to live and die and never come out of themselves—to never realize the possibilities hidden within themselves.

The greatest triumph in life is for people to discover themselves in Christ—to discover the rich, full happy life God created them for—then to let Him fully develop that unlimited life in them.

Only when **you desire** what **God desires** can He produce His dream in and through you.

*No good thing will he withhold from them that walk uprightly before him.*Psa.84:11

*I wish above all things that you may prosper and be in health, even as your soul prospers.*3Jn.2

*He satisfies the longing soul, and fills the hungry soul with GOOD things.*Psa.107:9LB

Forceful Ideas

In the Bible story of Nehemiah, when they decided that they should no longer live in poverty, inhibition and subservience, God placed **His ideas** in their hearts — ideas of freedom, of plenty, of security and of dignity as God's people.

This became so real to them that they decided to **require** total recovery and reestablishment.

When they **required** what God **inspired,** they **acquired** what they **desired.**

Look at what happened to them.

*They took strong cities and a fat land, possessed houses full of all goods, wells digged, vineyards, olive yards, fruit trees in abundance: so they ate, were filled, became fat, and delighted themselves in God's great goodness.*Neh.9:25

They had endured enough second class citizenship. They moved up, and they won.

Look at what God says, and remember, this is written in the Bible because it is for **you** as much as it was for them.

*I made an everlasting covenant, promising never to desert them, but only to do them good. I will put a desire into their hearts. I will rejoice to do them good, all the good that I have promised them.*Jer.32:40-42LB

*Fields will again be bought, deeds signed, sealed and witnessed. I will restore PROSPERITY to them.*Jer.32:43-44LB

That is what happens when you decide to **require** what God offers. Your decision, your commitment to His plan is the key.

*Commit your way to the Lord. Trust also in him and he shall bring it to pass.*Psa.37:5

Jesus said, *I have come so that you may have life, and that you may live in abundance.*Jn.10:10

God says: *Instead of shame and dishonor, you will have a double portion of prosperity and everlasting joy. All will realize that you are a people God has blessed.* Isa.61:7,9LB

Inherit the Earth Now

Religion "spiritualizes" God's blessings. It promises that when you get to heaven, you will be rich.

God's desire is that you *inherit the earth* Psa.25:13; 37:9,ll; Mat.5:5 — **now.** He created it for you to enjoy and to use **in this life.**

Faith with Purpose

We REQUIRE His **life** in order to share His love.

We REQUIRE His **power** in order to act as His ambassadors.

We REQUIRE His **health** in order to be at our best in life for Him.

We REQUIRE His **resources** in order to finance His programs.

We REQUIRE His **love** in order to serve humankind with His non-judgmental attitude.

We REQUIRE His **light** in our lives in order to spread His sunshine on the paths of others.

We REQUIRE His **inspiration** because we are His mouthpiece and we can only share the vitality that we draw from Him.

We REQUIRE His **authority** because we are authorized to speak and to act in His name.

We REQUIRE His **joy** and **enthusiasm** because we represent Him in a demoralized, dejected world.

We REQUIRE **what God has created** because He has entrusted us with His plan.

God Needs Us for His Plan

THE FIELDS God has entrusted to us are raw and wild and rich. But if we want to profit from them, we must use God's ideas and laws and cultivate them in order to make them productive.

THE RIVERS He has given us are flowing and free and powerful. But if we want them to serve humanity, we must use God's ideas and laws to tame them, harness them, dam them and make them the enormous benefactors God intended them to be.

THE MOUNTAINS He has created for us are strong and vast and priceless. But if we want to benefit from them, we must scale them, mine them, explore them and conquer them in order to realize their immeasurable wealth for humankind.

Unless we manage our emotions, perceive our unlimited potential and commit ourself to possess

God's best, our lives will be like wasted fields, untamed rivers, unconquered mountains.

A pastor complimented a farmer whom he was visiting. He reminded him of how God had blessed his farm and bestowed such abundance upon him and his family.

The wise old gentleman replied: "Yes, pastor, God has blessed our farm. But you ought to have seen it when God had it all by Himself."

Chapter 24

GOD'S HANDS
ARE YOUR HANDS

DURING THE second World War, a beautiful statue of Jesus, in France, was damaged. The villagers there loved their church and they affectionately gathered up the pieces of their statue, which stood in front of their sanctuary, and repaired it. But they never found the hands.

Some of the people said, "What good is our Christ without hands?"

That gave someone an idea, and he had a bronze plaque attached to the statue engraved with these words: **"I have no hands but your hands!"**

One day a visitor saw it and wrote a poem:

I have no hands but your hands,
  to do my work today.

I have no feet but your feet,
  to lead folks on the way.

I have no tongue but your tongue,
  to tell folks how I died.

*I have no help but your help,
to bring folks to my side.*

He Works Through Us

Jesus reaches out His arms and extends His divine blessings to people, **through us.** We are His body. His ministry in our community is expressed **through us.**

He will not send angels to do it. He functions **through you and me** now. If we are too busy with other things, if we think we are not good enough, if we feel our own affairs are more important, if we think we do not have time, then **our Christ is like that French statue; He has no hands.**

Day of Discovery

I shall never forget the change that took place in Daisy and me when we turned away from narrow and limited religious concepts, braved the tempest, released the past and discovered that we had been entrusted with God's plan in earth.

We were destined for His big kingdom business.

God had made **us** His partners.

There is no limit to what God can do through those who discover His plan.

Christ found a blind beggar and gave
him eyesight and a new lifestyle.

He found a leper and cleansed him
and gave him dignity.

He found a demon-possessed woman and made her His messenger.

He found a crazy, naked man and made him His representative to the ten cities of the Decapolis.

He found T.L. Osborn and Daisy Washburn, two farmer teenagers and sent them to over 80 nations together to minister to millions.

He has found you and He will develop His finest potential in you.

This Is Your Day

*Who may climb the mountain of the Lord and enter where he lives? Who may stand before the Lord? Only those with pure hands and hearts, who do not practice dishonesty and lying. They will receive **God's own goodness** as their blessing from him, **planted in their lives** by God himself their Savior. These are the ones who are allowed to stand before the Lord.* Psa.24:3-6LB

All God wants is for us to **desire** what He **desires.** Then He expects us to **have faith** in Him and to **believe** in His plan.

A great old gentleman came in a wheelchair to visit Daisy and me at our offices in Tulsa, Oklahoma. He held meetings in jails and prisons and won hundreds of souls.

Do you know what he wanted? A projector and our documentary crusade films. He was leaving to travel across America to show films and to tell people about Jesus. He is not a theologian, but he has God's idea about life.

He said, "I can't die. I can't die. I've got too much to do. Too many people are lost and need Jesus, and I must go tell them the Good News." **At 98 years of age, David Sizer did not consider that he had time to die.**

No one is too old and no one is too young. I was saved at twelve, began preaching at fifteen, was married at eighteen and became a missionary to India at twenty-one. **Today is your day.**

The Winning Team

When you make a commitment to God's plan, the Master Artist sculptures you until your finest potentials are discovered in full form.

You see yourself as God sees you. You see the unlimited possibilities that are in you. Nothing can stop you and God together.

God offers you everything to fulfill your happiness, prosperity, health and abundant living. *All things are yours, you belong to Christ; and Christ is God's.*1Cor.3:22-23LB

If you believe in God's plan, you can have whatever you desire and **require.**

*All things are possible to anyone who believes.*Mk.9:23

*The desire of the righteous shall be granted.*Prov.10:24

Delight yourself in the Lord; and he will give you the desires of your heart.^{Psa.37:4}

As God's offspring, we are not created to be nobodies.

*We are **heirs** of God, **joint-heirs** with Jesus Christ.* Rom.8:17

*We are **heirs** of the kingdom of God which he has promised to them that love him.*^{Jas.2:5}

We **are** what God **is** in us. We **require** what He has made available to us.

*As he is, **so are we** in this world.*^{1Jn.4:17}

Chapter 25

PRAYER OF DESIRE

THE PRINCIPLE of **desiring** God's blessings until you reach a place that you **require** them in order to be at your best with God, is vital to your faith.

To believe for something is to **desire** it. To have faith for something is to **require** it.

Prayer is our way to turn our **desires,** with our faith, toward God.

As I pondered THE POWER OF POSITIVE DESIRE expressed in prayer, I wrote this formula:

P — **Prepare** your heart by picturing God's abundant blessing.

R — **Require** these blessings by reaching out for them.

A — **Accept** God's ideas by claiming His best.

Y — **Yield** your taboos by saying "YES" to God's dream.

E — **Empty** yourself of negative influence by accepting His unlimited supply.

R — **Receive** His blessings by relating yourself to His plan.

Then you can turn your P-R-A-Y-E-R into a triumphant testimony for God's glory.

P — I have **POWER** because His presence is in me.

R — I am **RICH** because His resources are at my disposal.

A — I have **ALL** I need because He is at work in me.

Y — I say **"YES!"** to all of God's dreams because I am part of His plan.

E — I have **ENERGY** because He is invigorating me from within.

R — I am **RENEWED** because I am alive with His life and I share His purpose.

Help yourself to God's lifestyle.

To believe in God is to believe in good.

God wants good things to abound in your life. Never try to separate Him from His good life.

It is right for you to **desire** and to **require** the material blessings God has put within your reach, for you to prosper, to have a nice home that pleases you, to drive a nice car, and to have whatever good things give you pleasure.

It is right that your clothes look nice, befitting someone who walks with God, that you prosper and that your family enjoys the good life.

Require It—Have Faith for It

To REQUIRE God's best means you have **faith for His best.**

*Faith comes by hearing the word of God.*Rom.10:17

God's word informs you of His plan, of His promises and of His provisions for you. He has promised **every good thing** you can possibly **desire** or **require** in order to live a totally successful, happy and healthy life and to share that life with others.

Chapter 26

REQUIRE WHAT GOD DESIRES

THIS BOOK is written to free God's Spirit in you from the religious taboos of the past, so that your wings of desire can lift you to the level of your **desire**, for God's glory.

FREEDOM

REQUIRE **freedom.** It is inside you when you discover that God made you for unlimited greatness and total happiness. Let go of old ideas and old restrictions. Your mind and spirit are unlimited if you accept your release to dream new dreams and to achieve new goals.

God created you for freedom, and freedom for you.

Your desire for freedom is **God's desire** working in you so that the unique and wonderful **you** may be uninhibited, unshackled, unlimited in your potential as His representative.

From today, a new sense of God's freedom to explore His possibilities, will take wings inside you.

RICHES

REQUIRE **riches.** They are inside you when you discover all that God is and that He lives inside of you. Your *Acre of Diamonds* is on your own land. Dig for it until you discover the rich treasure that is locked up inside you. Set it free to produce the BEST in life for you.

God created you for riches, and riches for you.

Your desire for riches is **God's desire** working in you so that His plan can be fulfilled through you here on earth.

From today, God's wealth will begin to be multiplied in your life.

POWER

REQUIRE **power.** It is inside you when you discover who Jesus is in you, what ability the Holy Spirit of God has in you, the miraculous force of new ideas and dreams that you have when you set them into motion and apply the laws of success God has established.

God created you for power, and power for you.

Your desire for power is **God's desire** that His power be manifested in and through you to do His work.

From today, new power will be evident in your life.

HEALTH

REQUIRE **health.** It is inside you now when you discover that Jesus Christ has brought God's abundant life to you, that no sickness is in Him and that no sickness or weakness belongs in you, His body, which is the temple of the Holy Spirit.

God created you for health, and health for you.

Your desire for health is **God's desire** in you for His life and health to flourish in the body of His representative.

From today, new health will be manifested in your physical body.

SECURITY

REQUIRE **security.** It is inside you when you discover that God lives at your house, that His angels encamp around them that fear Him and that greater is He that is in you than he that is in the world.

God created you for security, and security for you.

Your desire for security is **God's desire** in you to prove His faithfulness, power, presence and companionship with you.

From today, a new consciousness of divine security will fill you.

PLEASURE

REQUIRE **pleasure.** It is inside you when you discover the wonder of being at peace with God, that all of the beauty and good of this world is created for you and that you are made for happiness, joy and exhilaration.

God created you for pleasure, and created the source of pleasure for you.

Your desire for pleasure is **God's desire** in you for total fulfillment.

From today, a new awareness of ecstasy and delight in life will be in you.

ACHIEVEMENT

REQUIRE **achievement.** It is inside you when you discover that God is at work within you, energizing you with both willingness and ability to accomplish anything that comes into your heart that is good for you, for people and for God.

God created you for achievement, and He created the laws of achievement for you.

Your desire for achievement is **God's desire** in you for success through you.

From today, you will achieve the dreams God puts in your heart.

FAITH

REQUIRE **faith.** It is inside you when you discover what God's plan is, what His promises are and that His word in you is like good seed that will produce of its kind once it is planted in good soil.

God created you for faith, and faith for you.

Your desire for faith is **God's desire** for you to have faith, and He is creating it in you by His word of promise so that you can live and experience the miracle life.

From today, new faith will begin to blossom in you.

LIFE

REQUIRE **life.** It is inside you once you discover that Jesus assumed all of your sins so that, as you believe in Him, He can come and live in you and impart God's divine life to you again.

God created you for life, and life for you.

Your desire for life is **God's desire** in you for His mighty, abundant life to pour through you as His new creation.

From today, God's life and His lifestyle will be yours.

STRENGTH

REQUIRE **strength.** It is inside you once you discover the force of Jesus Christ at work in you and the irresistible power of His Holy Spirit operating in and through you.

God created you for strength, and strength for you.

Your desire for strength is **God's desire** in you for His strength to be manifested in you to accomplish His dreams.

From today, new strength will equip your life.

GOOD PHYSIQUE

REQUIRE **a good physique.** It develops within you once you discover that your body is the temple of the Holy Ghost, the reflection of Jesus Christ, that you represent His royalty, and that you alone are in total control of your body, of what you do with it, of what and how much you eat, of whether you exercise and maintain fitness, and of how you dress as God's child.

You were created for a good physique, and the form of a good physique was His design for you.

Your desire for a good physique is **God's desire** in you for His very best form to be shaped in your body as His temple.

From today, a new resolve to shape up and to maintain your physique, for His glory, will motivate you.

GOOD LOOKS

REQUIRE **good looks.** It is a quality that expresses itself on your face, in your posture, in your eyes and through your behavior when you discover that Jesus is your real life, that your body is His and that you therefore express **His** peace, happiness, joy, positiveness, alertness, purity, love and delightful contentment.

You were created to look good, and the royal character that produces good looks is created for you.

Your desire for good looks is **God's desire** in you to let your countenance, your conduct and your attitude show the dignity and quality of a child of God.

From today, your new outlook and uplook will produce your new good looks as God's representative.

SUCCESS

REQUIRE **success.** It is inside you when you discover that, hooked up with God, you are a winner; that your idea source for success, your problem-solving ability, your persevering substance and your achievement power are all the expression of Christ at work in you.

You were created for success, and success is created and destined for you.

Your desire for success is **God's desire** in you for His new creation to succeed and win and excel.

From today, you will stop failing and start succeeding.

TRANQUILITY

REQUIRE **tranquility and peace.** It is inside you when you discover that Jesus Christ is your peace. There can be no fear of condemnation or guilt or judgment for any sin you ever committed, because He assumed it all in your place. You are at peace inside. Tranquility reigns in your domain.

You were created for peace, and peace is the domain that is created for you.

Your desire for this peace is **God's desire** working in you for His peace to flood your life so that no guilt, condemnation or judgment can ever threaten or spoil the harmony of God and you being together again.

From today, you will experience total peace.

COURAGE

REQUIRE **courage.** It is inside you when you discover that God's ideas in you are the best for all achievement; that God at work in you makes you a match for any task; that with God on your side, you can tackle any battle.

You were created for courage, and the power of courage is created for you.

Your desire for courage is **God's desire** in you for His representative to be aware of His presence and of His ability at work in you, every day.

From today, you will be a courageous believer.

LOVE

REQUIRE **love.** It is inside you when you discover that God is love and God, who **is** love, created you, so that makes you the product of love; therefore, you are made for love and love is your domain.

You were created for love, and love exists for you.

Your desire for love is **God's desire** in you for His love to flow through you to lift and to bless everyone, proving He lives in you.

From today, God's new, non-judgmental love will begin to rule in your life and to pour out to others through you.

HAPPY MARRIAGE

REQUIRE a **happy marriage.** It is inside you as you discover that God created male and female to make a complete team together; that with God's love in you, the camaraderie between two people united in marriage becomes a happy, blessed relationship and a holy delight shared for procreation, then for a lifetime of mutual friendship and fulfillment.

You were created for happiness in marriage, and the harmony and happiness of love in marriage was created for you.

Your desire for happiness in marriage is **God's desire** in you for harmony and the beautiful interrelationship which He envisaged for each male and each female He created.

From today, your marriage will be crowned with new and richer harmony and a happier companionship.

FRIENDS

REQUIRE **friends.** The ability to have friends springs from inside you when you discover that each human being is a God creature with the potential for being all that God is on this earth; which motivates you to interrelate with people objectively and to look for and to cultivate all that is potentially good, lovely, productive and virtuous in other human persons.

You were created for friends, and friends were created for you.

Your desire for friends is **God's desire** working in you for the companionship and fellowship of other God-created persons so that His goodness can be multiplied and His kingdom can prosper through His children carrying out His will on earth.

From today, you will see people with a new perspective and begin to share your life and gain new and deep friendships.

ESTEEM

REQUIRE **esteem.** It is inside you when you discover your own self-value, self-worth and self-dignity as a child of God, with His unlimited resources, ideas, abilities, attractions and values within you. Convinced of those virtues, your comportment, posture, outlook and conduct, motivates the highest esteem of others.

You were created for esteem, and the quality and nobility of God's esteem is invested in you.

Your desire for esteem is **God's desire** inside you yearning for the recognition and the honored respect He deserves in order for His plans and dreams on earth to be realized.

From today, as you conduct yourself in the capacity of God's representative, a new esteem for you will become evident.

ENERGY

REQUIRE **energy.** It is inside you when you discover the energizing influence and life-source of God at work in you, giving you worthy dreams, noble aspirations and inspiring objectives. These virtues develop a force of enthusiasm springing up inside you that pushes you with vigor and dynamic optimism.

You were created for energy, and energy was created for you.

Your desire for energy is **God's desire** in you for His recreated child to experience the dynamic life-force and enthusiasm which are necessary to the attitude of a positive winner in life.

From today, new energy and positive optimism will prevail in your life.

INFLUENCE

REQUIRE **influence.** It is inside you when you discover that the noble goals and worthy purposes of your life are to lift and heal and help and grow people. Your outreach and uplift to others lifts you higher and makes you stronger in your ability to improve and to strengthen your world around you.

You were created for influence, and the virtues which build influence into your life were created for you.

Your desire for influence is **God's desire** in you to see His children rise and rule and have dominion over this world He created for them. His plan must prevail and He has totally entrusted it to humankind.

From today, you will take your place as God's instrument on earth and you will begin to exercise a new influence for good in your world.

AUTHORITY

REQUIRE **authority.** It is inside you as you discover who you are in God's eyes, what He designed you to be, to have and to do; that you are heaven's representative on earth and that His source of ideas, secrets, solutions and laws put you in charge of any situation.

You were created for authority, and the laws of authority were created for you.

Your desire for authority is **God's desire** in you for His offspring to represent Him and His domain on this earth, prohibiting the domain of Satan; it is His desire in you to exercise the rule of His laws of freedom, success, health and happiness.

From today, you will begin to practice the awareness of who you are, and to exercise your right to master negative forces, and to possess your God-given empire.

INSPIRATION

REQUIRE **inspiration.** It is inside you as you discover the authentic vibrancy of the Jesus life in you which puts a smile on your face, a sparkle in your eyes, a spring in your step and optimism in your conduct. Everyone around you will draw inspiration from you.

You were created to inspire others and the ingredients and virtues for inspiration were created for you.

Your desire to inspire others is **God's desire** in you for His representative to be so happy, so peaceful, so objective, so decisive, so tenacious, so successful and so generous that everyone who meets you will be motivated to higher objectives and a higher lifestyle.

From today, you will experience a fresh power to inspire people around you and to improve your world.

REALITY

REQUIRE **reality.** It is inside you as you discover that God loves you, that He sent His Son to save you, that Jesus bore your diseases, your sins and your weakness, that He assumed your guilt and endured your judgment to redeem you to God as though you had never sinned, so that your new life, health, happiness and fulfillment are a reality that you know as well as you know that two plus two equal four.

You were created for reality, and the substance for reality was created for you.

Your desire for reality is **God's desire** in you to cause all the world to know that what you believe and possess is more than religion or superstition, humanism or mind science; that God is real, that His word is infallible, that His promises are sure, that His laws are workable, that redemption is a fact, that His life is actual, and that it comes into human believers and translates into the **reality** of peace, health, success and happiness.

From today, God's life and nature and laws at work in you will be a greater reality than ever.

Chapter 27

DESIRE-POWER
IS FAITH-POWER

IT IS YOUR trust in God's plan and in His abundant provisions that causes you to rise up inside, to fight off negating limitations and to say **I REQUIRE HIS BEST so that I CAN BE HIS BEST!**

That is faith-power at work in you.

The Bible says: *Anyone who comes to God must believe.*Heb.11:6

Jesus said: *Have **faith** in God.*Mk.11:22

Paul said: *Without **faith**, it is impossible to please God.*Heb.11:6

Faith means you link yourself with God, even when you cannot see Him or feel Him. Faith means you believe His promises, and you pray, and receive the answer in a way that no one can explain.

FIRST:
Faith Means That You Link
Your Littleness to God's Greatness

God who made the sun and the moon and the stars; God who made the birds and the flowers; that same God made you and He wants to reach out to bless you right now.

So, link your littleness to God's greatness. If He clothes the lilies of the field, He cares about you.

When Jesus took the children up in His arms to bless and to heal them, I think He was making a point that no one is insignificant in His eyes.

Religion may have made you feel unworthy and unimportant before the Lord, but relate your littleness to His greatness and believe that He cares very much about you, then ask for and **require** His best in life.

Remember the supreme price that God paid for you — His only begotten Son. He would never pay such a price for a "nobody." The fact that He paid so much to prove His love for you is eternal proof that you are really "somebody" in His sight. So relate yourself to Him and **require** His best — now.

SECOND:
Faith Means That You Link Your Need to God's Supply

The Bible says: *God shall supply all your need.*[Phil. 4:19] Whatever your need is, it will be supplied if you have faith in God and his promise enough to act on His principles and to require what you need.

Throughout the Bible the Lord met every need of those who believed on Him, whether those needs were physical, spiritual or material.

When a multitude was hungry, He broke a few pieces of bread and fishes and fed them all [Mk.6:35-42] and He does the same today.

A widow in the Bible showed her faith by taking her last meal and baking a cake for God's prophet, Elijah. Her meal and oil never diminished as long as the famine endured. God increased her supply by a miracle.[1Kg.17:10-16]

A widow walked four days to bring her sick son to our crusade in Kisumu. She had only a little meal in a can—enough for two days. She linked her need to God's supply and both she and her son ate from that meager supply all of the way to the crusade, for four days during the crusade and on her journey home. Friends told us later that she had more meal in that can when she got home than when she started her faith walk.

Link your need to God's supply and nothing shall be impossible. That is what faith means. You know God's best is created for **you.** It is **your** domain. You **require** it for your own good, then for the good of others around you.

THIRD:
Faith Means That You Link
Your Sickness to God's Healing

God said, *I am the Lord who heals you.*Ex.15:26 The Bible says: *He heals all of your diseases.*Psa.103:3 In the New Testament, Jesus always healed all who came to Him, and He has never changed. None are too sick. No one is too hopeless. He is the same today.

In one of our crusades they brought a helpless man who was a diabetic. The disease had progressed until he was blind. For some reason the man had also become insane, and was paralyzed so that he could not walk.

Someone carried him to our meeting and laid him on the ground near the platform.

I cannot explain how God does such things, but that night that dear man was healed. His mind was restored. His eyesight became normal. His paralysis left. He could walk, and run as well as I could.

Link your sickness to God's healing right now so that He can reach out to you and make you whole.

For nearly six decades, I have proclaimed God's promises in over 80 nations of the world. Everywhere, the same kind of miracles have taken place. What Jesus Christ has done for so many others, He wills to do for you if you reach out to Him. (Get my book, BIBLICAL HEALING.)

FOURTH:
Faith Means That You Link
Your Sins to God's Forgiveness

God says: *Call to me and I will answer you. I will cleanse you from all of your iniquities. I will pardon all of your sins that you have transgressed against me.* Jer.33:3,8 What a wonderful promise.

The Bible says: *Whoever shall call on the name of the Lord shall be saved.* Ac.2:21

There was a cruel witch doctor who attended our crusade in Nigeria. He listened to the gospel, he believed on Jesus Christ and was transformed by God's new life.

He came to the platform and wept as he talked to the people. He said, "I have been so evil and have spent my life putting curses on people. I have given them much poison and have even been the cause of the death of several people."

He said, "I did not know that God would love a wicked man like me." Then he added, "Now I am transformed. From now on, I will help people to have life instead of death."

That is what happens when anyone reaches out to God for His salvation. That is the life which is available to you, right where you are. Just link your sins to God's forgiveness and receive His pardon and transformation like that witch doctor did.

FIFTH:
Faith Means That You Link
Your Impossibilities to God's Possibilities

O Lord God! You have made the heaven and the earth by your great power and stretched out arm, and there is nothing too hard for you. Jer.32:27

Jesus said: *The things that are impossible with people are possible with God.* Lu.18:27

In one of our crusades a young man, Harold Khan, was brought, wearing a big brace on his left leg from his hip to his foot. The right leg was five inches shorter than the left one. His right shoe had a metal extension to help him walk evenly. The short leg was proportionately smaller in diameter than the left one.

That young man listened to the gospel and received Jesus Christ as his savior and Lord. (He had been raised in the Moslem faith.)

During the prayer, Harold was instantly healed. How it happened I do not know, but in one moment, his withered leg became the same size and length as the other one. This case is well known in the island nation of Trinidad, because Harold was treated in a government hospital.

Harold stood on our platform holding aloft his big steel hip-to-foot leg brace in one hand, and his 5-inch, built-up shoe in the other.

Both legs were exactly the same. It was a miracle.

The Good News is that Jesus Christ wants to do for you whatever you need, when you learn of His blessings as Harold did, and when you reach out to Him in faith.

Nothing Is Too Hard for God!

Behold, I am the Lord, the God of all flesh: Is there **anything** *too hard for me?* Jer.32:27

For with God **nothing** *shall be impossible.* Lu.1:37

Desire-power for the impossible, is faith-power that makes it possible.

That is why you can REQUIRE GOD'S BEST and you can ACQUIRE HIS BEST and you will BE HIS BEST.

Chapter 28

WHY REQUIRE THE BEST?

TO THE MOST unworthy person — a persecutor of Christians, a hater of the gospel: a man called Saul of Tarsus — God stretched out His hand and offered the rich and abundant life.

The Lord made three statements to Saul as he was en route to take as prisoners some Christians. A light shined from heaven and he fell to the ground.[Ac.9]

Here are three formidable statements:

FIRST: *I am Jesus.*[Ac.9:5]
What He meant was: I **DESIRE** YOU!

SECOND: *Now stand up.*[Ac.9:6]
That was to say: I'LL **INSPIRE** YOU!

THIRD: *You are my witness.*[Ac.26:16-18]
In other words: I **REQUIRE** YOU!

Jesus saves us, then He makes us His partners.

He redeems us then sends us out as His messengers.

He enriches us then makes us His good will ambassadors.

Your greatest personal development is to get God's view of the world, to see people as God sees them, to absorb His nature and to get in harmony with His emotions until He lives and loves and lifts people through you.

That is why you **require** His BEST.

You give up your small ambitions and you aim for the **top.** The basic attitude in achieving all success is:

> **See a need and fill it;**
>
> **See a hurt and heal it;**
>
> **See someone lost and guide them to the light;**
>
> **Find someone down and lift them up.**

That spells **"mission"** for every human being — reaching people, carrying out God's plan for good in this world.

Every life that is on target with God has a **divine mission** and therein lies **the reason for us to require God's best in life.**

This is the way I spell MISSION:

M — Making new roads; seeing the possibilities for good in our world and making new roads and making things happen for the betterment of humanity.

I — Inventing new solutions; seeing the needs and the problems of humanity, and inventing new solutions to those problems, and new ways to meet those needs.

S — **Saving new souls;** seeing the waste of human lives without God; saving new souls through the loving life-force of Jesus Christ at work within us and through us.

S — **Sowing new seeds;** seeing the unlimited potential of every human person and sowing new seed-ideas of success and of happiness in people's minds to help them become their best for God.

I — **Inspiring new discoveries;** seeing the depravity and the incurable loneliness of people without purpose, and inspiring new discoveries of their roots in God, so that they can be the "somebody" that God created them to be.

O — **Opening new doors;** seeing the loss of productivity in those who are locked in with their poor self-image, and opening new doors to the unlimited fulfillment of loving service to others.

N — **Nourishing new dreams;** seeing the destructiveness of negativism, of helplessness and of hopelessness, and nourishing new dreams of positive living by the infusion of faith in God and miracle living in Jesus Christ.

Those noble objectives spell God's true MISSION for us.

To accomplish those goals, we REQUIRE God's BEST.

Faith in God is the most positive force in humanity. Doubt, fear and unbelief form the most negative and destructive force that a person can experience.

The finest spiritual achievement—the deepest spiritual level of Christianity can be summed up in four steps:

Self-discovery – *know who you are;*

Self-development – *reach out to others;*

Self-discipline – *make Jesus Christ your standard;*

Self-fulfillment – *reproduce yourself in others.*

The greatest achievement on earth—the greatest mission of the believer is to reach out to human beings:

*To **see** in them God's dignity;*

*To **breed** in them God's worthiness;*

*To **seed** in them God's lifestyle;*

*To **sell** them on who they are;*

*To **tell** them what Jesus Christ wants to be in them.*

*To **give them the gift** of eternal life;*

*To **give them the lift** of worthwhile living.*

To accomplish these ideals, we **require the good life,** and I assure you that **the good life is God's IDEA for YOU!**

Accept it now.

Say: "**YES!** I require His BEST."

Say: "I am able, because God in me is able. I am created in His image. He lives in me. All that I **require** is **Him** at work in me."

Say: "God who gives me a dream, helps me realize that dream. Nothing is impossible to **me,** because nothing is impossible to **Him.**"

Dr T.L. and Bishop LaDonna Osborn minister across ten major cities of the ex-Soviet Union, proclaiming the miracle-producing gospel to packed auditoriums in every city, and giving a full set of Osborns' 10 books to each adult.

SECTION V

PERSPIRE

PAUL CALLS IT the fight of faith. I use the word PERSPIRE, because it rhymes with the other words I chose for this book, and it expresses the principle of **believing what God says despite everything contrary.**

God wants **to be reassured of your faith in His plan.**

So **perspire,** if need be, but never **retire.**

Never quench the **fire.**

Never get stuck in the **mire.**

Require what God **desires.**

And you'll **acquire** what you **desire.**

Persist until you get it. **Perspire** (if need be), hang on until you KNOW that you **are** and **have** and **can do** what God wants in and through you.

Chapter 29

GOD'S FAITH
AT WORK IN YOU

THE POWER OF POSITIVE DESIRE, when activated by God's promises, is really **the force of faith** at work in you.

When you want what God wants, then your ambition, your desire, your drive to possess it is **God's faith at work in you.**

The Bible consistently teaches that God wants our daily reassurance that we believe in Him, that we trust His word, that we will never bow to any other influence than His, that we commit our lives to the integrity of His word above everything else in the world. **That is faith.**

God Never Changed His Mind

When Adam and Eve doubted God's word and believed Satan's lie, the basis of faith for God's plan of friendship was gone. He could not share His lifestyle with disloyalty. Light could not dwell with obscurity, nor faith with deceit, nor loyalty with betrayal.

Satan knew God could never compromise the honor of His word.

Man and woman made their choice to believe a lie and to distrust God's word. They deteriorated in slavery and died. All generations were infected by their sin.

The Magnanimous Idea

But God never changed His mind about wanting people as His friends and co-workers.

Love had the magnanimous idea of legally redeeming humankind, by offering a perfect substitute to assume *our* guilt and to suffer all judgment for *our* sins. That substitute was Jesus Christ.

When we commit ourselves to **believe** that Christ did this for us, God accepts us back into His family.

To come back to God, all He wants is our reassurance that we will never do as Adam and Eve did, that we will not disavow His integrity by doubting what He says.

Paul calls it *the fight of faith.*[1Tim.6:12] I use the word PERSPIRE, because it rhymes with the other words I chose for this book, and because it expresses the very vital principle of **believing what God says despite everything that may seem to be contrary.**

Jesus said: *Have faith in God.*[Mk.11:22]

*Without **faith** it is impossible to please God; for anyone who comes to God must believe.*[Heb.11:6]

Say "Yes!" to God's Success

I recorded a 2-tape cassette album on the subject: YES TO GOD'S SUCCESS. (You may request that
album for yourself.)

The Lord inspired me with a poem about
SUCCESS.

*Declare a "YES!" to God's SUCCESS
    And then CONFESS that you POSSESS;
You'll be BLESSED with the Father's BEST,
    As you PROGRESS with His NOBLESSE.*

*That's the reason that I STRESS
    The vital TEST to know you're BLESSED;
It's to CONFESS that you POSSESS,
    And that says "YES!" to God's SUCCESS.*

*I say "YES!" to God's SUCCESS
    When I CONFESS that I am BLESSED.
Then I POSSESS what I CONFESS,
    As I EXPRESS I have His BEST.*

*I don't MESS and I don't GUESS,
    For nothing LESS than God's own BEST
Is mine UNLESS I get OPPRESSED.
    I know I'm BLESSED with God's SUCCESS.*

*Now I'm so glad I'm not DEPRESSED.
    God set me free from all DISTRESS.
And thru' His word I've been IMPRESSED,
    So I say "YES!" to God's SUCCESS.*

Once you have committed yourself to go for
life's **best,** STICK TO YOUR DREAMS. Set your

goals as high and as big as God's ideas are, and as vast as His resources are.

Do more than just **inquire** and **admire; aspire** and even **require** God's good things.

Be so committed to desire what God desires, that you persist until you get it; that you **perspire** (if need be), that you hang on until you KNOW that you **are** and **have** and **can do** what God wants in and through you. **That is faith in God.**

Chapter 30

IN BIG BUSINESS
WITH GOD

JESUS SAID: *Seek first the dominion of God and your right standing in it.*Mat.6:33

Jesus taught us to affirm, every time we pray: *Thy kingdom come. Thy will be done.*Mat.6:10

That is what the virgin, Mary, did. She said, *Be it done to me according to your word.*Lu.1:38

You say: **Yes, Lord, let Your kingdom be realized in me; let Your total will be accomplished in me. Work in me Your pleasure. Let Your abundance be multiplied in my life.** *Your kingdom come! Your will be done.*

God's kingdom in **you** is BIG BUSINESS. God has **big** ideas. You are born for the **big** life. You are hooked up with **greatness.**

Abandon forever the dingy, judgmental, guilt-ridden ranks of the defeated. Walk out into God's **big** world of **full** living, and **exuberant** health, of

His **abundant** life and **creative** thinking, of His **positive** lifestyle and **productive** involvement.

God **saves** you, then makes you His **partner.**

Believe in **your** salvation enough to believe in your partnership potential with deity. Believe in your **destiny for greatness.** Believe in your **dynasty of desire.**

Your Father Says, "YES!"

We were praying about this book. We knew that God wanted us to **lift** you so that He could **gift** you.

The presence of Jesus Christ flooded into our prayer chamber like the warm glow of the morning sun. It seemed that every color of the rainbow brightened our room.

I believe the Lord spoke to me about this book, and about you as His teammate.

Beautiful Bible verses about His abundance and goodness poured into my spirit.

His divine power has given to us ALL THINGS that pertain to LIFE.[2Pet.1:3]

Then His voice seemed to say in every ray of that rainbow of light:

"YES! YES!

"Tell people, I say, YES!

"What you desire, I desire.

"YES! I want you blessed.

"YES! I want you complete.

"YES! I want you healed and strong.

"YES! I want you prosperous and successful.

"YES! I want you fulfilled.

"YES! I want your dreams fulfilled.

"Tell the people, YES! I say, YES!"

Whatever things you desire, when you pray, believe that you receive them, and [YES!] *you shall have them.* Mk.11:24

If you can believe, [YES!] *all things are possible to you.* Mk.9:23

Yes to Your Dreams

God's abundance is for YOU! But He wants you to DESIRE it, to **inquire** about it, to **admire** it, to **aspire** to it, to **require** it, and to **perspire** (if the going gets tough) to possess it.

It is your **empire**—your **dynasty of desire**. It is **your DOMAIN**. It is **God's kingdom within you.**

All you have to do is to **only believe** His word, to **only trust** in His plan of love, **to reaffirm your faith** in the face of any roadblock of accusation, condemnation or guilt that is put in your way.

Reaffirm your faith and trust in God enough to **perspire,** if need be, to prove to Him that you are committed to His ideals.

Set your goals. **Seek, knock, ask.** Then stick to it when the going gets rough because, even when your faith is tested,[1Pet.1:7] you know that God says "YES!"

He says, *Whatever you ask in my name,* [YES!] *I will do it.*[Jn.14:13]

Ask, and [YES!] *you will receive it, that your joy may be full.*[Jn.16:24]

Jesus used three words:

1. ASK — Be specific.

Don't ramble in your aspirations. Sight your target. The Living Bible says, *You will be given what you ask for.* Asking requires a response. God always responds. *Call to me and **I will answer you.***[Jer.33:3]

2. SEEK — Go for it.

Put action to your aspirations. If you need a job, apply. If you need knowledge, get it. If there is something you can do, do it.

3. KNOCK — Be persistent.

Someone will open the door if you knock. God is the opener of every door. He says "YES!" you can have it. I created it for you. It is **your** domain.

Anything is possible if you have faith.[Mk.9:23]

Don't You Quit!

I read this poem somewhere and I think it was
written for you.

When things go wrong as they
    sometimes will,
When the road you're trudging
    seems uphill,
When the funds are low and the
    debts are high,
And you want to smile, but you
    have to sigh,
When cares are pressing you
    down a bit,
Rest if you must, **but don't you quit!**

Life is strange with its twists and
    turns,
As all of us sometime must learn.
And many a failure turns about,
When we might have won had we
    stuck it out.
Don't give up, though the pace
    seems slow,
You may succeed with another blow.

Success is failure turned inside out,
The silver tint of the clouds of doubt.
And you never can tell how close
    you are,
It may be near when it seems so far.
So stick to the fight when you're
    hardest hit—
It's when things get worse that
    you must not quit!

Chapter 31

OATH OF PROSPERITY

TRUE FAITH can only be based on God's plan, His ideas, His dream. These are recorded in His word.Rom.10:17

All that He wants from you is your daily reassurance that **you believe** Him enough to stick to His desires regardless of the influences or circumstances stacked against you.

If your faith is suppressed by negative teaching that to desire better things and a better life is wrong, then you will waste your life and die in resignation and pious failure.

You will be like so many who have bound themselves with an oath of poverty. God never planned for anyone to do that. He planned prosperity.

It would be good if you would decide today to take an OATH OF PROSPERITY and say:

"I VOW never to be poor and indigent again, since my Father created the wealth of this planet for me to enjoy.

"I VOW *never to be unable to reach out
and lift others in need. God is in me
and He is rich.*

"I VOW *to always appropriate God's BEST
in life so that I can enjoy His abundance
myself, and so I can share His abundance
with others in need.*"

The Lord is my shepherd; **I will not want.** *My cup
runs over.*Psa.23:1,5

That is the lifestyle for which God created you.

Love-Power Creates God's Best

Dare to break with the bondage of religious negativism. Desire God's good things — His BEST in life.

Desire has been called the fire that produces the heat which generates the steam of your will.

When your desire joins with God's desire and your will blends with His will, then His love-power begins to create life's best in you.

Let a deep resolve form inside you which says:

*I am through with failure, mediocrity,
sickness and poverty.*

*I am through with jealousy, resentment,
fear and guilt.*

*I am through with loneliness and
disappointment, with bills and
unpaid mortgages.*

The fire of desire is burning in you for a better life, better health, more love, greater success, a closer relationship with God, prosperity, peace and happiness.

Recognize that those desires are God *working in you to will and to do His good pleasure.*[Phil.2:13]

Chapter 32

CHOOSING
WHAT GOD DESIRES

WHEN DAISY AND I were only 20 and 21 years old, we sailed for India with our ten-month-old son. We believed that the people there needed to know Jesus Christ more than the people in our country. There were so many millions of them who had never heard of God's love for them, and there were only a few messengers to tell them.

We knew God **wants** every human person on earth to know how He loves and values them.

We desired what God desired. But the enemy was not planning to let us realize that desire.

We were there for nearly one year. We could not convince the Hindus and the Moslems that Jesus Christ was the Son of God, that He is risen from the dead and that He lives today. We did not understand about God's miracle-working power.

We had no way to prove to them the current evidence of God's love. It was written in the Bible, but we could not give them living proof that the Bible is God's word.

The Living Proof is What Counts

Salvation is based on the fact that, *if you believe in your heart that God raised Jesus from the dead, and if you confess with your mouth that Jesus is Lord, you will be saved.*Rom.10:9

We could not convey that message because, without miracles, there was no tangible evidence to prove that Jesus Christ had risen from the dead. So we came home.

But we had seen the masses who were without the knowledge of what Jesus Christ had done to redeem them to God, and we would never be the same again.

We had reached the **perspiring** stage. Was God's idea workable? Could we accomplish what He wanted done? Did we believe in it enough to stick to it?

We prayed and fasted. We were determined to find the way to carry out Christ's commission. We knew He could only do His work through people.

People tried to pacify us. They encouraged us to get on with life and to give up our passion to share God's goodness with the world.

We were told that those millions were accustomed to their fate and misery, that they were happy with their own religions, that we should forget about those millions abroad and get on with evangelizing our millions at home.

Yes, we had to **perspire.** But we were so convinced of God's love for everyone that we never budged from our goal.

Jesus Came to Our House

One day, we heard a woman preach at a great camp meeting. Her subject was, "If You Ever See Jesus, You Will Never Be the Same Again."

The next morning at 6 o'clock, Jesus Christ came into our bedroom. I saw Him like I would see anyone that walked into our room. I lay there helpless in His presence. I could not move a finger or a toe. Water poured from my eyes, yet I was not conscious of weeping. I learned that the human body cannot stand the presence of Jesus.

After a long while, I was able to move myself and I lay on the floor, face down. That afternoon, when I walked out of that room, I knew I was a new man. I knew I was not proclaiming a dead religion. I was proclaiming a living Jesus. I knew that this world wanted to know that He is really alive.

From that day, the fire of our desire burned brighter. We had a lot more **perspiring** to do, but we knew that we had found the secret to convincing the non-Christian masses that Jesus Christ is the same today as He ever was.

Everyone Is Welcome

Since that overwhelming experience, we have, ministered for almost six decades in over 80 nations of the world, proclaiming Christ out on great fields, stadiums, parks and public places, so that all people of all religions can hear the gospel and know how God loves them.

Out under the canopy of the skies they come by the scores of thousands to hear the couple from a foreign land, who teach from a book they call the Bible. They love hearing the wonderful things about God's love, about His power and about His plan to give them health, peace, happiness, success and self-esteem.

All over the world, we have seen the same results People always react in the same positive, grateful way when they hear God's love-plan and see the proof that He is alive and that His promises are good **today.**

But in every land, religions are busy putting people down, emphasizing their unworthiness, demeaning their human status, exacting and enjoining self-reproach and penance, deifying suffering, heaping accusations, motivating guilt, threatening damnation and, in general, demoralizing them with condemnation, despair and hopelessness.

God's Goodness in Human Persons

Religionists invariably begin their approach by emphasizing that **people are BAD.**

Humanism begins its approach with the opposite philosophy, that **people are GOOD.**

Both miss the point.

The message of the Bible is not to emphasize either that **people** are good or bad, but that **GOD is good** and that **His goodness** can be imparted to people when they believe in His love-plan.

The Christian message is to share God's love-plan so that people can be restored to Him and have His goodness restored to them.

Desiring **that** is **desiring what God desires.** Desiring it so intensely that you will brave any opposition and stick to that dream at any cost, **is FAITH.**

Knowing how God loves everyone, regardless of their race, color or status, causes you to reject limitations, to refuse inhibitions, to resist opposition and to align yourself with His dream and to go for the summit.

Chapter 33

EVERYONE MEANS
YOU'RE THE ONE

GOD WANTS **you** to be happy, healthy, prosperous, successful and fulfilled, with real living and genuine self-esteem.

I believe the Lord inspired me with these lines, to help make this vital point:

> YOU'RE the one
> He had in mind
> When Christ returned
> For humankind.
>
> It's EVERYONE
> He came to find
> So YOU'RE the one
> God has in mind.

We have given of our best to share God's dream with millions of people. It is to extend His plan to **you** that I am writing this book. It will increase the fire of desire in you until you go for His BEST in life.

Never succumb to the cheap, sanctimonious doctrine that **you** are a nobody, that **you** are born for mediocrity, that **you** must be patient in poverty, that **you** must accept your commonality.

Anyone Can Go to the Top

Always remember that **you** are born for **royalty,** for **greatness,** to be a **partner** with God, to live in **plenty,** to **prosper,** to **succeed,** to **reach out** as God's representative, **to go to the top** and to **lift others** with you.

God's promises to **you** are abundant.

If you live in me and I live in you, **you** *can ask whatever* **you desire,** *and it will be done to* **you.** Jn.15:7

Whoever *calls on the name of the Lord will be saved.* Rom.10:13

Whoever *believes in me shall have eternal life.* Jn.3:16

Everyone *who asks receives.* Mat.7:8

I gave a television address and titled it, EVERYONE MEANS YOU'RE THE ONE. I was inspired to write a poem about it for you.

> *When you've begun to know God's Son,*
>   *And comprehend what He has done.*
> *Your enemy is overcome*
>   *By the blood of God's own Son.*
>
> *T'was shed for YOU — for EVERYONE*
>   *Who comes to God. The battle's won.*
> *You'll marvel; He helps ANYONE*
>   *For He tells EVERYONE to come.*
>
> *What God has done for ANYONE*
>   *He wills to do for EVERYONE.*

The work is done; the Son has come,
  EVERYONE means YOU'RE THE ONE!

His Word can't fail, and that's no pun.
  For Satan's work has been undone.
God's promise is for EVERYONE, and
  EVERYONE means YOU'RE THE ONE!

That is why, even if you must **perspire** under the heat of pious resistance or condemnation because you reach for the better life, go ahead and **perspire — but never stop —** until you **acquire** what you **desire.**

No one is too poor to prosper; no one too sick to be healed; no one too helpless to get up; no one too condemned to be forgiven; no one too beat down, disparaged and dejected to rise on the freed wings of desire and soar to the better life.

Chapter 34

KARIUKI
THE KIKUYU

I CAN NEVER FORGET Kariuki, the Kikuyu maniac who ran across the hills of Kikuyuland for 17 years, practically nude and demented, clutching rubbish in his arms, running from one village to another, putting it down and desperately gathering more objects in his deranged preoccupation with debris and worthless rubble.

A young Christian believer reached out to him in the kind of love that sends you to the top. He conceived a way to entice Kariuki into his pickup, in order to bring him to the crusade.

Out on the crusade field, among thousands of people, the believer stood beside Kariuki who was still clutching his armful of rubbish. We were entirely unaware of them being in the crowd as we taught about God's love that day.

Of all the great miracles that we have witnessed across the world — and we may have seen as many or more than any couple has ever been privileged to see—practically all of them have taken place out on the field, amidst the people, without us knowing anything about the need or the miracle until it had already occurred.

Kariuki was one of them.

The Miracle of Seed Power

Our God is in His word, like life is in seed. When the seed is planted in people, it produces of its kind.

The healing seed of God's healing promises, heals people.

The miracle seed of His miracle promises, produces miracles in people.

His seeds of self-esteem and of personal value create a harvest of self-value and of self-wealth in the lives of people.

The saving seeds of God's love-plan produce salvation in people.

That day we taught about God's love-plan and about how He values people. After the teaching, as we prayed for the multitude, the Spirit of the Lord came upon Kariuki in a way which I cannot explain. In a moment of time, the tormenting evil spirits left him and he was well and normal.

The believer realized that Kariuki was really healed, and brought him to the platform to tell the multitude what had happened.

His tattered clothes did not cover his nudity. His hair was long, matted and full of fleas. His beard was long. His body emitted a terrible odor.

But I could see that this man had been visited by the Lord.

The Transforming Power of Love

I took him by the shoulders and said, "Kariuki, you just look beautiful." That lifted him and helped avoid embarrassment for his indecent appearance before the people.

I said, "Kariuki, you are my brother. My Father and your Father is the same. We are one." I pulled him to me and embraced him, then I looked at him again.

I said, "Kariuki, I am so proud of you. My Father created you. He has a plan for you that nobody in the world can carry out as well as you can. You are going to go places." Then I embraced him again.

Then he talked to the people and gave the most intriguing report of how he had lived in tormented compulsion to run from village to village, gathering debris. He was amazed at the miracle he had received and thanked everyone for their prayers and for their love.

I told some of the pastors to provide him a hot bath, to get his hair and beard trimmed, to buy him clothes and a beautiful necktie, to get him a Bible and to bring him back.

The Miracle on Display

The next day, Kariuki was sitting on the platform. You would have thought he was one of the ministers. In fact, he never failed to sit next to Daisy on the platform during the rest of the crusade. He always had a happy expression on his face and was always anxious to tell anyone about his miracle.

In each meeting, I would ask Kariuki to publicly read, for me, the scripture lesson which would be the basis for my teaching. He had learned to read, prior to his insanity, so his lecture was a beautiful witness of God's love for people.

Winners Around the World

Around the world, millions of human lives are wasting in the dirt—sitting, waiting, withering, dying:

Not growing, but groveling;

Not producing, but procrastinating;

Not building, but wilting;

Not self-sustaining, but self-condemning;

Not attaining, but complaining.

The noble and beautiful desire of our lives is to salvage human beings, to give them **self-discov-**

ery, to teach them **self-development,** to help them in **self-discipline,** to inspire them for **self-fulfillment** and to motivate in them **self-esteem.**

Our **desire** is God's **desire;** it is to show people His love, to tell them the price He paid for them, to inform them of their value to Him, to show them the way to find Him.

Our desire is to lift people...

By new faith in God,

By new faith in themselves,

By new meaning in life,

By new dreams to inspire them,

By new ideals to live by,

By new purposes to accomplish.

We **know** that is **God's desire,** so we are committed to success in order to fulfill His dream as His co-workers. Even when we must **PERSPIRE** to press through the profusion of prejudiced resistance to reach our goals with God, **we do not quit—we are WINNERS.**

Chapter 35

WITH GOD
ALL THE WAY

THE EMPIRE of desire can never be realized if you dramatize the impossible and fail to harmonize the possible.

To hocus-pocus the dream so much that you never focus the beam, or release the steam and increase the gleam, is futile.

We can turn every opportunity into a possibility when we **desire** what we **admire** and **require** it enough to **perspire** for it (if need be) in order to **acquire** it.

I like a little poem I saw somewhere because it lifts the spirit and helps one to **desire** the best and to **perspire** (when necessary) to **acquire** it.

"Bite off more than you can chew
    Then chew it.
Plan for more than you can do,
    Then do it.
Point your arrow at a star,
    Take good aim and there you are.

Arrange more time than you can spare,
   Then spare it.
Take on more than you can bear,
   Then bear it.
Plan your castle in the air,
   Then, with God's help, you are there!"

The apostle Paul said it very succinctly: *Run that you may* **obtain. Strive** *for* **mastery.**[1Cor.9:24-5LB]

He Is at Work in Us

Jesus said: *My kingdom is like a merchant on the lookout for choice pearls.*[Mat.13:45LB] *It is like a treasure hidden in a field, which when a person finds it, he or she sells everything and buys that field.*[Mat.13:44]

With God at work in us, energizing us by His life and love and power, we are unlimited in our potential for success and fulfillment. We are destined for happiness and then to overflow in blessing to others.

We gain by giving.

We live by loving.

We are lifted by lifting.

We reap by sowing.

We increase by sharing.

We are blessed by blessing.

We get so "turned on" by the people possibilities around us that we will not permit any person or system or condition to prevent us from achieving our desire with God.

Perspire but Never Retire

We know that *God is a rewarder of those who diligently seek him.*[Heb.11:6]

We know that *He who has begun a good work in us will perform it.*[Phil.1:6]

When the going gets rough, when the pious criticism and sarcasm gets heavy, when condemning accusations are heaped against you, remember all that God wants of you is **to be reassured of your faith in His life-plan for you and for others.**

So **perspire,** if need be, but never **retire.**

Never quench the **fire.**

Never get stuck in the **mire.**

Desire what God **desires.**

You will **acquire** what you **require.**

Jesus said, *All things which the Father has are mine.*[Jn.16:15] You can say the same thing. *All things are yours, you are Christ's; and Christ is God's.*[1Cor.3:22-23]

Jesus said: *The Father who dwells in me, he does the works.*[Jn.14:10] You can say the same thing. *God is at work within you, giving you the will and the power to achieve his purpose.*[Phil.2:13PHLP]

All that God **is,** is at work in **you.** He is the only power that exists, and He is in you. **So never put limits on Him by limiting yourself.**

Literally, you can do *all things* through Christ who strengthens you ^{Phil.4:13} – through Him who is at work in you.

You'll Get What You Go For

You are in bondage to no one. The only restrictions that can ever hold you back are those which you give power to, by your own choice.

No one else can take God and His power away from you.

To repeat what Berton Braley said:

> *"If you want a thing bad enough*
> *To go out and fight for it,*
> *Work day and night for it,*
> *Give up your time and your peace*
> * and your sleep for it,*
> *If only desire of it*
> *Makes you quite mad enough*
> *Never to tire of it,*
> *Makes you hold all other things*
> * tawdry and cheap for it,*
> *If life seems all empty and useless*
> * without it*
> *And all that you scheme and you*
> * dream is about it,*
> *If gladly you'll sweat for it,*
> *Fret for it,*
> *Plan for it,*
> *Lose all your terror of God or man*
> * for it,*

If you'll simply go after that thing
  that you want,
With all your capacity,
Strength and sagacity,
Faith, hope and confidence, stern
  pertinacity,
If neither cold, poverty, famished
  and gaunt,
Nor sickness nor pain
Of body or brain
Can turn you away from the thing
  that you want,
If dogged and grim you besiege
  and beset it,
You'll get it!"

That is why I love what Robert Collier said back
in 1948.

**Be not afraid to stand boldly out,
crying: I want this, and I am going to
have it! It is my rightful heritage, and
I demand it!**

*According to your faith it will be done to you.*Mat.9:29

Say to yourself: **God created me. He values me.
He loves me. He paid for me. He redeemed me.
He is in me.**

Then add this: God not only **made** me and **loves**
me; God **needs** me. God has a **plan** for me. God is
depending on me.

Everything Is Right!

Religions try to block that discovery. They teach
you that you are **not good** enough, **not spiritual**
enough, **not deep** enough.

Society says, you are **not educated** enough, **not smart** enough, **not rich** enough, **not gifted** enough, **not old** enough, **not young** enough.

People say your **color** is not right, your **race** is not right, your **background** is not right, your **location** is not right.

But the fact is, that you have **everything right** because **you are God's idea** and **you are one-of-a-kind.**

God's big kingdom business is entrusted into **your** hands. You are not going to fail, because you are committed to Him and He is at work within you.

*You never chose God. He chose you.*Jn.15:16

*He is the vine. You are one of his branches.*Jn.15:5 The kind of life-stuff that flows out of Him, flows out of you.

*The works that he does, you do also.*Jn.14:12

*All things are possible to you because you are a believer in him.*Mk.9:23

With God in you, **it is "YES!" all the way!**

If you have to, *you can say to your mountain, remove from here and it shall remove; and **nothing** shall be impossible to you.*Mat.17:20

The Osborns' message is the good news of what Jesus Christ did for YOU when He died, in your place, on the cross.

He assumed the judgment of your sins in order to restore you to God as though you had never sinned.

No crime can be punished twice. No debt can be paid twice. He acted on your behalf. Now you have FREEDOM to become all that He has in mind for you.

SECTION VI

ACQUIRE

LIFE IS NOT being in TRACTION; it is being in ACTION.

Life is not ASPIRING; it is AC-QUIRING.

All you **know**, all you **hear**, all you **believe**, all you **hope** for and all you **aspire to** is an **unpossessed domain until you decide to ACQUIRE it and commit yourself in ACTION to get it.**

Once aware of God's dream, desire what He desires **enough to commit yourself to what He says. Decide to ACQUIRE it and ACT accordingly.**

You can **ACQUIRE** whatever you **desire.** Let THE POWER OF POSITIVE DESIRE, be released into ACTION. It is time for you to **possess your domain.**

Chapter 36

ACQUIRING IS ACTING

YOU HAVE MOUNTED five golden steps toward your empire of desire.

Now this sixth section will place you on the fertile plateau of **your domain with God** and it will help you to take your rightful place in His plan for your life.

At this strategic level, God has another vital secret to share with you. With it, the total domain of His abundance is at your command. But it depends on your knowing and using the secret.

You ask: "What is the secret?"

It is just one word—like a password. It is the vital secret of **ACTION.**

You have now risen to this exhilarating level because...

1st You began to INQUIRE and to discover how full the Bible is of God's Good News.

2nd As you looked, you ADMIRED His abundant goodness and decided it must have been created for you. Who else?

3rd Deep inside, you ASPIRED, you yearned for this good life, for fulfillment and for satisfaction.

4th You decided that you REQUIRED God's best in order to succeed in His love-plan.

5th You made up your mind to PERSPIRE, if necessary; to fight for it, to resist opposition and to gain your prize.

6th Now you are ready to ACQUIRE what you have desired.

It is time to use **the secret of ACTION.** It is time for you to take what you want.

There is no real **faith** without ACTION.

There is no real **hope** without ACTION.

There is no real **love** without ACTION.

There is no real **life** without ACTION.

Time to Possess Your Domain

Faith without works [action] *is dead.* Jas.2:17,26

If someone is naked or hungry and you say, Depart in peace, be warmed and filled; but you do not give them what is needful, what does it profit? Jas.2:15-16

*Remember, this is a message to **obey,** not just to listen to. So don't fool yourself. If you **just listen** and **do not obey,** it is as though you see your face in a mirror and walk away and forget what you look like. But if you keep looking steadfastly into God's law for free people, you will **do what it says,** and God will bless you **in everything you do.*** Jas.1:22-25LB

You are like God's people were, when they had crossed the wilderness. They had fought through the opposition and had held fast to their dream of God's good land that belonged to them. At last it was time to ACQUIRE the land.

Then the Lord sent His message to them:

Behold, the Lord your God has set the land before you: GO UP AND POSSESS IT. Fear not, neither be discouraged. Deut.1:21

The Israelites **acted** on the word of the Lord to them and they ACQUIRED the land. **They possessed the domain which belonged to them and by their action, God was able to bless them in all that they did.**

There comes a time when we must prove to God **by our action,** that we **trust** Him and that we **believe** in His plan.

The Commitment to Win

Once we are aware of God's dream, there comes a time when we must **prove** that we desire what

He desires **enough to commit ourselves to act on what He says.**

Jesus saw a crippled man who had been unable to walk for 38 years.

God wanted that man to be healed. But did the crippled man want to be well?

Jesus asked him: *Do you desire to be made whole?*
Jn.5:6

He asks that of you, now.

Are you dissatisfied with life as it is? Do you **want** a better way? Do you **desire** a fuller life? Are you **willing** to be prosperous and successful and to assume the responsibility of administering wealth and success?

The crippled man blamed others for his 38-year plight. He said that no one would help him to get well.

Jesus said, in essence: **Help yourself. Get up. Carry your bed. Walk.**

The man got up and walked and was whole again.

That is what God says to you and to me.

Decide what you **desire** and GO FOR IT. You can **have** or **do** or **be** anything that you **desire.**

Chapter 37

INSPIRED TO ACQUIRE

THROUGH IDEAS and aspirations which God plants in you in seed form, He desires to produce the harvest of abundance in you that was His original dream for you.

The message of Jesus Christ is good news.

*You are the **salt** of the earth.* Mat.5:13-14

*You are the **light** of the world.* Mat.5:13-14

*Follow me and I will **make you.*** Mat.4:19

*Your sins are **forgiven.*** Mk.2:5; Psa.103:3

*Rise up and **walk.*** Lu.5:23 Never hang your head in shame again.

***Stretch forth** your hand.* Mk.3:5

Only believe. Lu.8:50

Have faith. All things are possible. Mk.9:23

He gives hope to the hopeless and power to the powerless. He is good to all who come to Him and who call upon Him. Desire the good life.

This principle of desire is vital because your **action** is motivated only by what you deeply aspire to.

When there is no desire, no **choice** is made, no **decision** is taken — no **action** is performed.

Without the "want to" there is no "will to."

Jesus Supplied It— You Can Acquire It

Let the real Jesus stand up in you and come alive. Whatever He is, He is **in you.**

Everyone He touched was made better, richer, healthier, more successful.

> **He touched** lepers and they became clean.Mk.1:41
>
> **He touched** blind eyes and sight was restored. Mat.9:29
>
> **He touched** crippled and lame people and they walked.Mk.6:55-56
>
> **He touched** weary and demoralized people and they received new life.Mat.14:26
>
> **He touched** people who had fever and they became normal again.Mat.8:15
>
> He **touched** people who were afraid and they were confident again.Mat.17:7
>
> He **touched** deaf mutes and they could hear and speak.Mk.9:25
>
> He **touched** wounded people and they were instantly healed.Lu.22:51

That is what He yearns to do in your life. But His touch always involved **action** on the part of the one in need.

We simply **get up and go into action,** and then we possess the good land which God has created for us.

Chapter 38

OMUKHULU
FROM NYANZA

FOLLOWING one of our African crusades, one of the national ministers went into an unreached area to share the gospel.

He encountered a tragically pathetic man in a village who was crippled by paralysis and had been abandoned to die. His name was Omukhulu.

He had fallen 45 feet and had crushed his lower vertebrae and his hip structure.

Surgeons performed numerous operations, trying to reconstruct his bones but there was no improvement, and he seemed more helpless than ever.

His case was hopeless, so he had been put out of the hospital and sent back to his village to die.

Years of despair had dragged by, until Omukhulu's two brothers and his father had tired of waiting on him and had abandoned him in a mud hut. His mother brought a bit of food to him but even she came seldom because everyone agreed that he would be better off dead; if he was abandoned, he would die sooner.

Our Message Brought New Hope

The young minister found him alone in despair, and brought him new hope and a new life.

Our crusade messages had been interpreted into the Kiswahili language which Omukhulu spoke, so the minister took some of the cassettes of our teaching to him, and loaned him a cassette player with new batteries.

We had taught about putting **faith into action.** I had related Bible verses about **acting faith** and had talked about the crippled man whom Jesus told **to get up and walk,** and about the man with a withered hand to whom Jesus said, **stretch it out.**

We had recounted many examples of people who had attended our crusades, who had believed on Jesus Christ, who had received Him as savior, and who had **put their new faith into action** and had received great miracles.

Day after day, Omukhulu listened to those cassettes. He believed on Jesus Christ, repeated the prayer I had directed, and had been saved.

At the end of our teaching, we had led the multitude in a prayer for physical healing.

I had emphasized the Bible verse: *This is the confidence that we have in him, that if we ask anything according to his promise, we know that he **hears** us, and if we know that he hears us, we know that we **have received** what we asked him for.*[1Jn.5:14-15]

They Acquired It When They Acted on It

I had told the multitude that if they believed God had heard their prayer, then it was time to put their faith into **action** — to **do** whatever they had not been able to do before.

If they had not been able to see, I had told them to open their eyes, to look, to expect to see.

If they had not been able to walk, I had told them to do as Jesus commanded the cripple; to arise and to walk. If they had used braces or supports or canes or crutches, I had told them to remove them or to toss them aside and to walk, expecting God to restore them.

I had told them **to ACT according to their faith.**

Mighty miracles had taken place in that meeting. The blind had received sight. Deaf people had received hearing. Many who had been hopelessly paralyzed, lame and crippled had put their faith into action and had been miraculously healed.

We had invited all who had received miracles to come to the microphone and to share their miracle publicly for the encouragement of others.

Scores of miracles had been reported and everything had been captured on the recordings.

Omukhulu Got the Message

Omukhulu had lain there on his straw mat on the earthen floor of his hut, listening to our teaching, to the prayers and to the miracles — over and over. He had become a believer.

Finally, one day, he said to himself, **"I have listened enough! Now I must pray, as the people did in that Osborn Crusade, and God will answer me like He answered them."**

He turned the machine off and there, alone, he had begun to pray. He could not remember how long he had cried out to the Lord.

He says that all of a sudden, he had this idea: **"I have prayed enough. I do not need to act as a beggar. It is time for me to act as though God has answered me, like Mr. Osborn told the people in the crusade to do."**

He was at the same place you are at right now.

You have **inquired** and **admired** enough.

You have **aspired, required** and **perspired** enough.

It is time for you to **ACQUIRE** whatever your heart **desires**. It is time for THE POWER OF POSITIVE DESIRE, based on what you know God desires, to be released into ACTION. It is time for you to possess your domain.

Enough Listening—
Enough Praying

Omukhulu shoved the cassette player out of his way and he pushed himself upward with his arms, expecting to get up and to be whole. Nothing happened.

He repeated his effort. No change.

He dragged himself to the wall of his hut and propped his shoulders against it, maneuvering every possible way he could to lift himself. If he gained a few inches, he slumped back.

He was determined to get up. He had believed the message. He **desired** what God **desired.** He never succumbed to uncertainty or to fate. He kept **acting** his faith.

Under the steaming heat in his African village, he became drenched in perspiration. He never abandoned hope. He knew what He believed. He was certain that God's promises were true. **He trusted God's integrity.**

As he floundered on the dirt floor that afternoon, he had bruised his head and arms, hitting them against nearby objects.

Sweating, struggling, crying to God and doing everything he could think to do, he again inched his shoulders up the wall with his head, when suddenly a beautiful presence filled the hut.

Acquiring God's Miracle Power

Omukhulu said, "A soothing warmth entered the top of my skull and spread through my head. It was like a warm liquid as it moved down my spine and into my hips. As it spread, every nerve and muscle came alive. My bones were recreated."

Omukhulu said: "I got on my knees, then I stood up. I was perfect. I raised one leg, then the other. They were whole. I looked up to God and I wept and laughed hysterically for a long time. I could not control my joy.

"The more I realized what had happened, the more I was overcome with joy.

"Then—I thought of my people. I went out of my hut and began running, throwing my arms in the air, yelling as loud as I could to everyone, that it was me, Omukhulu, that I was healed.

"As I ran and yelled, amazement swept through the village."

Was It Omukhulu—
Or His Ghost?

"When I came near my father's hut, my brothers and my parents saw me, but they fled as my mother screamed: 'It's Omukhulu's ghost!'

"I ran after her and dragged her to the ground. With my face soaked in sweat and tears of joy, I held her and I said, 'Mama, it's me! I'm Omuk-hulu. The living God has healed me through Jesus Christ. Don't be afraid of me. Mama, I'm your son. I'm healed. Look at me. Feel of me. It's your son, Omukhulu.'"

The dear old lady finally realized that she was in the loving embrace of her own son whom she and her family had abandoned to die.

Omukhulu reminded her of the minister who had brought to him the recorder and the cassettes of the crusade at Kisumu. She realized that her son had become a believer in Jesus and that the living God had done a miracle.

The Vital Secret of Action

I could recount hundreds of miracles as wonderful as this one is, which we have witnessed in our crusades around the world. (Get our book THE GOSPEL ACCORDING TO T.L. AND DAISY which contains 512 pages of firsthand accounts of the miracle power of Jesus Christ in our lifetimes.)

I have shared Omukhulu's story to illustrate how vital it is to reach the level of ACTION.

All you **know**, all you **hear**, all you **believe**, all you **hope** for and all you **aspire to** is an **unpossessed domain until you decide and commit yourself to action.**

It is time for you to say, as Omukhulu said, **"I have listened enough. I have read enough. I have inquired, admired, aspired, required and perspired enough. It is time for me to ACQUIRE the good life that God has created for me. I shall arise and go possess my land. I demand it. It belongs to me."**

One translation of James 2:17 is: *Believing is useless without **doing** what God **wants** you to do.*

You can go in His name and:

Turn problems into **opportunities,**

Turn impossibilities into **possibilities,**

Turn disgrace into **dignity,**

Turn fear and insecurity into
   peace and tranquility,

Turn defeat and weakness into
   authority and victory,

Turn poverty into **prosperity,**

Turn deceit and betrayal into
   integrity and fidelity,

Turn selfishness and hatred into
   charity and a new beginning in love.

Chapter 39

FAITH AND ACTION

ONCE YOU COMMIT yourself to ACQUIRE God's best, once you step into the arena of action, God will begin to materialize His blessings in your life.

It is great to have faith, and it is even greater when you put **action** with that faith.

You are born to have faith and **you** are born for **action.**

1. With faith in God, and the confidence to **act** on His dream, **you win with Him.**

2. With faith in God's dream, and the confidence to **act** on His word, **you and God build a life worth living.**

3. With faith and **action, you set goals** and **reach them.**

4. With faith and **action,** you **motivate yourself** and the **people** around you.

5. With faith and **action,** you **overcome adversity** and come through **smiling** and **shining** and **winning.**

6. With faith and **action,** you **conquer self-defeating habits.**

7. With faith and **action,** you use your time profitably and become an **investor,** a **producer** and a **harvester.**

8. With faith and **action,** you exercise the power of choice; you **choose right** and **win every time.**

9. With faith and **action,** you **discover self-confidence based on God-confidence.**

10. With faith and **action,** you are **free of fear.**

11. With faith and **action,** you are **enthusiastic.**

12. With faith and **action,** you **prosper** when it seems impossible.

13. With faith and **action,** you are **loved, cherished** and **valued** by people.

14. With faith and **action,** you **lift, help** and **heal** people.

15. With faith and **action,** you **turn stress into strength.**

16. With faith and **action,** you **manage your life** rather than being manipulated.

17. With faith and **action,** you **live with courage** and **happiness** 365 days a year.

18. With faith and **action,** you **love everyone** and have no enemies.

19. With faith and **action,** you **transform problems** and **tough times** into **opportunities** and **blessed times.**

20. With faith and **action,** you **see rainbows** when others see only storm clouds.

21. With faith and **action,** you are **an optimist** instead of a pessimist.

22. With faith and **action,** you **hear music** when others are deaf to life's songs.

23. With faith and **action,** you **soar and discover new worlds** that others would view as forbidden and foreboding.

24. With faith and **action,** you **sing** when others are suffocated by gloom.

25. With faith and **action,** you **reach** and **touch realms** that others do not even believe exist.

26. With faith and **action,** you **acquire** what most people only wish for.

27. With faith and **action,** you discover that Jesus is literally **at work in you,** continuing to do **through you** what He began to do when He walked this earth in Bible days.

28. With faith and **action,** you **discover new possibilities** in life and **you utilize them.**

29. With faith and **action,** you **challenge the impossible** and **you turn it into reality.**

30. With faith and **action,** you are **free of the tradition** that enslaves you.

31. With faith and **action,** you **think new thoughts** which no one ever thought before.

32. With faith and **action,** you **experience adventure,** you **explore** and you **conquer.**

33. With faith and **action,** you find **needs** and **you meet them.**

34. With faith and **action,** you find **hurts** and **you heal them.**

35. With faith and **action,** you find **problems** and **you solve them.**

36. With faith and **action,** you do the same things Christ does. You and He share the same lifestyle, the same goals, the same love-power, the same abundance. *The works that I do shall you do also.* Jn.14:12

Chapter 40

YOU ARE GOD'S HEADQUARTERS

YOU ARE VALUABLE to God. **You** are His partner in life. His life is for **you,** for **your house,** and for everyone under **your influence.**

** Link your *confidence* to God's *providence.*

** Be an *achiever* because you are a *believer.*

** You have *creativity* because of God's *credibility.*

** There is no *clout* whenever you *doubt.*

** There is no *relief* where there's *unbelief.*

** You will only *rust* if you fail to *trust.*

** But you will *climb* when you get God's *mind.*

** It will light your *fuse* when you believe the Good *News.*

1. Jesus turned the **toughest problems** into the **greatest possibilities.**

2. He used the **worst sickness** to demonstrate the **greatest healing.**

3. He transformed the **most lowly sinner** into the most **wonderful saint.**

4. He made of the **most tragic sorrow,** the opportunity to show His **greatest compassion.**

5. He turned the **most impossible situation** into the most **glorious success.**

6. He took **tough Peter** and made him a **compassionate leader.**

7. He transformed a **common village woman** into a **witness of His mercy.**

8. He delivered a **devil-possessed woman** and made her a **messenger of His resurrection.**

9. He so changed a hated **tax collector** that God used him to **record one of the Gospels.**

10. He is at work, right now, **transforming you into His headquarters for blessing, happiness, success and abundance.**

Chapter 41

LEARNING THE
BIG SECRET

AFTER WE SAW JESUS, Daisy and I had faith to tackle anything. We had so many ideas which were new and creative. We put **action** with them.

At that time no one thought of going out on an open field, in a NON-Christian country, calling together witchdoctors, lepers, maniacs and the masses of people, to share with them the teaching of God's love. We have won multitudes ever since.

No couple has yet lived who has taught the Jesus life to as many millions of non-Christians, face to face, in as many nations, nor has witnessed as many great healing miracles and conversions among those people, as Daisy and I have done.

Action Is the Password

We learned early in life that **action** is the key. Our lives have been overwhelmingly happy, productive and fulfilled. Our abundance has overflowed to millions of others.

Our example of success and happiness in mass miracle evangelism has ushered in a new era of soulwinning evangelism, out in public places where the people live and work and play. The idea has swept across practically every free land in the world.

What we have **desired,** we have **acquired,** because we have put **action** with our **believing.**

Did you ever hear the story of the three little chicks who got up one morning?

And the first little chick
  With a cute little shrug
Said, "I wish I had me
  A nice fat bug."

The second little chick
  With a funny little squirm
Said, "I wish I had me
  A nice fat worm."

The third little chick
  With a funny little squeal
Said, "I wish I had me
  Some nice yellow meal."

Look here, you three,
  Said the hen in the patch,
"If you're ever going to eat,
  You'd better learn to scratch!"

Not in Traction but in Action

Daisy, my wife said to me one day:

Life is not by LUCK, but by PLUCK.

THE POWER OF POSITIVE DESIRE

It's not by a lucky NUMBER, but by a
written WONDER.

It's not by CHANCE, but by STANCE.

It's not a HAPPENSTANCE, but an
INHERITANCE.

It's not by OPTION, but by ADOPTION.

It's not by one's SELECTION, but by God's
ELECTION.

It's not a DRAWING OUT, but a CALLING
OUT.

It's not by NUMBER, but by MEMBER.

It's not being in TRACTION, but being in
ACTION.

It's not ASPIRING, but it's ACQUIRING.

SECTION VII

INSPIRE

OSPEL spells INSPIRATION.

G — For the **Greatness** God gives us,

O — For the **Opportunity** He offers us,

S — For the **Success** He plans for us,

P — For the **Positiveness** He puts in us,

E — For the **Excellence** He breeds in us,

L — For the **Love-life** He gives to us.

Look at Jesus Christ. Contemplate the wonders of His life and the love which He shares with us. That spells **INSPIRATION**.

When you look up and see Him standing in your boat, you stand up too. You are strong. You grow tall. The Jesus life in you INSPIRES others too.

Nothing is as **inspiring** as to know that God is at work in our lives. Jesus said, *The Father in me does the work.*

Chapter 42

THE LIFE
THAT INSPIRES

DAISY AND I were privileged to experience together over five decades of fabulous living, exciting love, unparalleled success and inspired ministry to millions in almost 80 nations.

Scores of times we have been asked: "How do you stay so enthusiastic, so inspired and so inspiring in your ministry?"

Many times, people have said: "You seem 'turned on'. Each miracle you witness seems as thrilling to you as the first one must have been!"

We walk with the wonder-worker, and you do too. The Jesus life is a living reality at our house. Now, it is at your house too.

Jesus said: *I am come that you might have life.* Jn.10:10

John said: *Anyone who has the Son, has life.* 1Jn.5:12

Alive In Jesus Christ

We are INSPIRED because we are A L I V E.

A — We have **Ability** — God is at work in us.^{Phil.} ^{1:6LB} He is at work in you too.

L — We have **Liberty** — Jesus is free in us and we are free in Him. ^{Jn.8:32,36} You have His freedom too.

I — We have **Identity** — We count with God. We are royalty. We are family. We bear His name.^{Rom.8:14-17} You share that identity too.

V — We have **Vitality** — We are turned on to God. We have energy. We have enthusiasm.^{2Tim.1:7} You have that vitality too.

E — We have **Equality** — Equality with God. Equality with Jesus.^{Gal.4:17LB} You share that equality too.

** We are **equal to circumstances.** Jesus in us can meet any situation and handle it.

** We are **equal to problems.** Jesus in us is big enough to solve any difficulty.

** We are **equal to responsibilities.** No job is too difficult for Jesus and us to accomplish together.

** We are **equal to possibilities.** There is no limit to the goals we can achieve with Christ.

** We are **equal to people.** We are not inferior to anyone. Jesus, in us, makes us the BEST there is.

Being ALIVE spells being INSPIRED, and we live to **inspire** others.

We can only give what we have.

The Gift of Inspiration

When we look at Jesus Christ and contemplate the wonders of His life and the love which He shares with us, we are **INSPIRED.**

David was so **inspired** by life as a God-person that he wrote psalms which have lifted the hearts of humankind for centuries.

He drew his inspiration from the marvel of God's creation: He said, *The Lord has made people a little lower than "God,"* [King James Version—than *"angels;"* Original Hebrew, French and certain other languages—than *"God."*] *And crowned them with glory and honor. The Lord gave them dominion over the works of his hands; He put all things under their feet.*[Psa.8:5-6] No wonder we are **inspired.** No wonder we **live to inspire** others.

Chapter 43

THE WONDER
OF A HUMAN PERSON

THERE IS NOTHING on earth as awesome and as potentially powerful as a human being made in God's likeness.

There is a legend in Japanese literature that underscores this point.

A Japanese stonecutter had worked year after year with his hammer and chisel, sculpturing figures out of stone—until his hands became rough and scarred.

The Stonecutter

One day he was depressed. He thought: "I'm a nobody. I'm just a stonecutter—just a human being."

As he sat there, a shadow passed across him. It was the king on his great white stallion, looking so powerful with his soldiers marching with him.

The king moved on, but the stonecutter was so inspired that he wished he could be the king. He began to sing: **"The king! The king! I wish I were the king!"**

Be the King!

He heard a voice say: "THEN, BE THE KING!"

Suddenly he felt a crown of gold placed upon his head. He was seated upon a beautiful white steed. Soldiers were at his side as he marched in regal power.

But the hot sun bore down upon them. Some of his soldiers fainted and dropped. Even the king dismounted, almost overcome.

Reeling under the heat, he asked: "Is anything more powerful than the king?"

The voice answered: "YES, THE SUN!"

Be the Sun!

So he began to sing: **"The sun! The sun! I wish I were the sun."**

The voice said: "THEN, BE THE SUN!" And he was—powerful, strong—sending his rays across the earth and the sea, transforming the water into great billowing clouds which blocked out the sun so that it could not send its powerful rays to the earth.

Then he asked: "Is anything more powerful than the sun?"

The voice said: "YES, THE CLOUD!"

Be the Cloud!

He sang: **"The cloud! The cloud! I wish I were the cloud."**

The voice responded: "THEN, BE THE CLOUD!" And he was.

He arose in great billowing masses across the earth, releasing torrents of water which drenched the earth and formed great rivers whose mighty torrents rushed down mountainsides, carrying everything in their wake, plunging toward the sea.

As the waters crashed against a great boulder, it resisted the force, splitting the waters before they could pass.

He asked: "Is anything more powerful than the cloud?"

The voice replied: "YES, THE ROCK!"

Be the Rock!

So he sang: **"The rock! The rock! I wish I were the rock."**

The voice said, "THEN, BE THE ROCK!" And he was—unshakeable, irresistible solid granite. But he looked up and saw someone coming toward him, chisel and hammer in hand.

He asked: "Is anything more powerful than a rock?"

The voice said: "YES, A PERSON!"

Be A Person!

So he sang: **"A person! A person! I wish I were a person."**

The voice spoke and said, "THEN, BE A PERSON!"

He looked and **saw himself,** a stonecutter, with his wrinkled, rugged hands. In one was a chisel, in the other a hammer. **Suddenly he felt the power of who he was.**

He arose to his feet and said: **"There is nothing as powerful as a human person with a living soul."**

Since we are made in God's image, we would say, "There is nothing as INSPIRING as the realization that we are created like God, *a little lower than himself, crowned with glory and honor, having dominion over all the works of his hands,* chosen to represent Him on earth,[Psa.8:4-6] filled with His love-power, reaching out and lifting people in His name.

That spells **INSPIRATION.**

Chapter 44

GOD'S IDEAS
INSPIRE ME

THE KINGDOM OF GOD is within us.

God created us.

Adam and Eve betrayed God's trust.

But God never gave up on His idea.

Jesus redeemed us, making it possible for us to come back and to be one with Him again, to have His kingdom in us so that He can rule through us again. That **inspires** me.

The cross means that God trusts us. He believes in us. That **inspires** me.

John said, *Here is love; not that we love God but that he loved us and sent his Son to be the sacrifice for our sins.*[1Jn.4:10] That is **inspiration!**

The Cross of Christ Inspires Me

When we look at the cross, we are inspired like John was, who said: *Behold, what manner of love the*

Father has bestowed on us that we should be called the children of God.[1Jn.3:1] That **inspires** me.

Everything Jesus did and said was to **lift** and to **inspire** people. That is why His message was **good** news.

The object of His coming was to uplift and bless, to heal and save people, to make inspired "some-bodies" out of downtrodden "nobodies."

Jesus Came to Inspire You

In the first sermon Jesus ever preached, He announced, *The Spirit of the Lord is on me, because he has anointed me to preach good news to the poor.*[Lu.4:18]

We were poor and desolate; we could not help ourselves, heal ourselves nor forgive ourselves. Then Jesus came to lift us and to give us hope, faith, love — and **life.**

For generations, the people had lived under the threatening dogmas of religionists. But Jesus came with **inspiration.**

No more sentence of **failure,** but destined success.

No more **penalty** of death, but the gift of life.

No more **fallen natures,** but redeemed new creatures.

No more deadly **sinfulness,** but Godly righteousness.

No more **lost sinners,** but saved winners.

The Source of Inspiration

When Jesus came, He **inspired** people with His **life,** His **love** and His **compassion.**

1. JESUS CAME to a woman with an issue of blood, who had suffered for twelve long years, and whom nobody wanted around. He said, "YOU are my daughter. YOU are loved. YOU are made whole!"

That is **inspiring.**

2. JESUS CAME to the demoniac who ran naked among the tombs, cutting his body with stones, menacing everyone he met. Jesus said, "YOU are important. I can use YOU. I shall clean you up, then YOU can be my messenger."

That is **inspiration!**

3. JESUS CAME to a woman taken in the act of adultery. Men were picking up stones to kill her. He said, "I forgive you. You can live a clean life. You never need to be condemned or guilty."

That is **inspiration!**

Jesus Christ does not want to put you down. He wants to **lift you up.**

He does not want to focus on your problem. He wants to **give you a solution.**

He does not want to call you a sinner. He wants to say, **"Your sins are forgiven."** He wants to lift and to **inspire** you so that your life can become His **inspiration** to others.

4. JESUS CAME to a woman who was bowed over and could not straighten up. He put His hand on her and said, "You are a daughter of Abraham. You should not be stooped over like this. Straighten up, Madam, and stand erect like the lady you are!"

That is **inspiration.**

God wants no one bowed or stooped or embarrassed. He comes to say, "Sir, Madam, stand up straight. Pull yourself to your full stature, and be what I have made you to be."

5. JESUS CAME to a cripple at the pool of Bethesda who had tried for 38 years to be cured. Jesus said, "Friend, if you want to be well, I want you to be well. Rise, pick up your bed and walk."

That is what I call **inspiration.**

6. JESUS CAME to say to **you** right now, "You need not be sick. You need not be condemned. You need not be poor. You need not be down on yourself."

7. JESUS CAME to say to **you,** "You can be forgiven. You can stand up tall. You can walk straight. You can be healed. You can prosper. You can have life's best. You can go to the top."

8. JESUS CAME to the thief on the cross. He said, "Friend, today, you can be with me in paradise. You can have real life."

That is **inspiration** and that is His message to **you.**

9. JESUS CAME to say to **you,** "My Father loves you and I love you. You can pray to Him in My name, without any ritual, and He will give you what you desire."

That is **inspiration.**

Under the oppressive yoke of religion, to just pray would have been sacrilegious. One needed to bring an offering to the priest and pay for an animal or fowl sacrifice.

His Teaching Inspires Me

But Jesus said, *Ask, and you shall receive; seek, and you shall find; knock, and it will be opened. Every one that asks receives.*Mat.7:7-8

That is **inspiration.**

Out on the hillside one day, He lifted the people and gave them self-esteem. **Nine** times He said, *You people who are listening to me can be beautiful, you can be happy.* (It was His beatitudes.)

BLESSED are you who are poor.

BLESSED are you who mourn.

BLESSED are the meek.

BLESSED are you who hunger and thirst.

BLESSED are the merciful.

BLESSED are the pure in heart.

BLESSED are the peacemakers.

BLESSED are the persecuted.

BLESSED are the abused and falsely accused.^{Mat.5:2-12}

Just imagine how different His teaching was from what they had been accustomed to hearing.

Jesus sat there and smiled, repeating His uplifting message **nine different ways.** In essence, He was saying, **"My friends, you can be happy; you can be beautiful; you can have fulfillment; you can have peace."** What a message! Not a putdown, but a lift-up — an **inspiration.**

He is saying to you: **"You are important. You count in God's plan. You have purpose."**

Chapter 45

GOSPEL MEANS INSPIRATION

TODAY IS A NEW DAY. We have a new way to come to God—the Jesus way—a new relationship with Him, a new faith, a new lifestyle, a new message, a new attitude toward God. It is called **good news.**

I wrote this gospel acronym and made it my subject for teaching at a recent convention:

G — for the **Grace** of Jesus Christ;

O — for the **Object** of His coming;

S — for the **Simplicity** of believing;

P — for the **Power** of childlike faith;

E — for the **Esteem** God has for you;

L — for the **Lifting power** of His dream.

That describes **INSPIRATION.**

For nearly six decades already, we have proclaimed that gospel to the world, telling people everywhere:

If you are poor, you can be **lifted up** and
made rich in Christ;

If you have sinned against God, you can be
forgiven;

If you are sick, you can be **healed;**

If you are down, you can **get up;**

If you think you are a nobody, God thinks
you are **somebody;**

If you are living in mediocrity, God wants
to give you **prosperity.**

Inspiring Good Around the World

All over the world, we have seen people come
and receive the wonderful message of Jesus Christ,
and be blessed and changed forever.

* Nations have been affected.

* Presidents, premiers, Governors, commission-
ers and mayors have welcomed our teaching
and have been lifted, with the people.

* Broken families have been reunited in new love.

* Alcoholics and chemical dependents have been
totally cured.

* Politicians have risen to greater success and esteem.

* Women have discovered new values and risen
to uncharted levels.

* Men who were, in fact, beggars now own their
businesses.

* University students have acted on the inspiration of the gospel and are now successful in leadership.

* Married women have become business owners, executives, entrepreneurs.

* Poor people now live good, prosperous lives.

* Incurable sicknesses have been miraculously healed.

* The deaf, the dumb, the lame and the blind have been healed.

* Cancers, tumors and all sorts of incurable maladies have disappeared.

* Defeated people have regained self-respect and self-esteem.

* Loneliness and fear have been lost in the glow of new faith and purpose.

* Thousands of people today are walking miracles. They are witnesses of the remarkable changes which have been experienced by those who have heard us teach these truths.

The object of this section in this book is to project in you the picture of the wonderful you that God created and to **inspire** you to hold that vision until, by His miraculous power, you become all that you see by faith.

I Am Inspired by
What I See in Christ

I see so much to be **inspired** about when I see Jesus Christ hanging on the cross, in my place. I know He did that so that He can bless, lift, heal and save me so that I can bless, lift, heal and save someone else.

The miracle essence of God's plan for you and for me, is: **He saves us, so that He can make us His partners in saving others. That is inspiration.**

1. **When I look at the cross,** it shows me how **VALUABLE** I am to God.

2. **When I look at the cross,** it shows me how much God **WANTS** me.

3. **When I look at the cross,** it shows me how much God **TRUSTS** me.

He believes that if someone tells us what He did for us on the cross, we will believe it, and will let Him come to us and remake us into His class of being.

It is great to talk about trusting God; but **what inspires me** is how God is trusting us.

It is great to think about what Jesus is worth; but **what inspires me** is when I think about what you and I must be worth. You may not think you are worth very much, but you are worth what God paid to save you.

It is great to talk about having faith in God; but **what inspires me** is to think about how much faith God has in us. He created us like Himself, then when we disappointed Him, He paid to restore us back to Him. That is reason for **inspiration.**

Gospel Lifting Power

Here is another gospel acronym which Daisy, my wife, was inspired to write, to encourage people:

G — for the **Greatness** God gives us;

O — for the **Opportunity** He offers us;

S — for the **Success** He plans for us;

P — for the **Positiveness** He puts in us;

E — for the **Excitement** He gives us;

L — for the **Love-life** He imparts to us.

This is your day to stand up taller, to walk with self-esteem and to be all that God designed you to be.

Chapter 46

THE WAY TO INSPIRATION

TAKE THESE five steps:

1ST **Be honest with yourself.** Realize that you are created to be like God. But sin poisoned your life. No power on earth can change you, except the life and love of Jesus Christ. So repent and believe the gospel and receive God's love.

2ND **Discover yourself.** Give God's dream a chance, so that the wonderful YOU which God made can come alive, and be happy, invigorating, inspiring and uplifting.

3RD **Commit yourself to God.** Determine to achieve the lifestyle that is honorable instead of dishonorable, that has fame instead of shame, that is constructive instead of destructive, that is gleaming instead of demeaning, that is **inspiring** instead of retiring.

4TH **Value yourself.** You are made in God's image. You are part of His plan to lift the world around you. You are unique. You are made for success and health and happiness. **God** needs you.

People need you. And **you** need you — the wonderful you that God has made.

5TH Invest yourself. Plant yourself in God's love, by giving yourself to Him and to His plan; then by reaping God's blessings which abound in you when you bless those around you.

These steps spell **inspiration** and **real living.**

Living the Inspired Life

Believing the gospel means that you live the **inspired** life.

You are **inspired** because you are *a laborer together with God.*[1Cor.3:9]

You are **inspired** because *Christ in you is the hope of glory.*[Col.1:27]

You are **inspired** because *you can do all things through Christ who strengthens you.*[Phil.4:13]

You are **inspired** because *if you ask anything in his name, he will do it.*[Jn.14:14]

You are **inspired** because when you believe on Him, *the works that he does, you do also.*[Jn.14:12]

You are **inspired** because you are sent out, in His name, **to give His message of love to all the world and to accomplish His miracles.**[Mk.16:17-20]

Believing the gospel means that you are Christ's messenger to the people of your world.

It means that you are an **ambassador for Christ** [2Cor.5:20] and that **you have His authority.**[Lu.9:1]

That is reason for **inspiration.**

The Way of Inspiration

You are inspired by three great facts:

1ST GOD VALUES YOU.

Look at Jesus on the cross. You realize the value God places on you by observing the price He has paid for you. He created you. He esteems you. He knows the "stuff" He has put in you. You are first class all the way.

2ND GOD TRUSTS YOU.

He trusted that if He would give His Son to die for you, you would realize that you have infinite value to Him; you would quit condemning yourself by destroying your own life and you would respond to His trust by receiving His life in you.

3RD GOD NEEDS YOU.

You ask, "Dr. Osborn, does God really need me?"

Yes. He can only carry out His work through you and me.

Jesus died for our sins. He was buried. He arose from the dead. He ascended to the Father. Then He came back to us, and when we are born again, **He comes to live in us.** Then He sends His Holy Spirit to empower us.

We are the body of Christ,[1Cor.12:27] the temple of the Holy Spirit.[1Cor.6:19] So God **needs** us.

God depends on us.

Our hands are His hands. Our eyes are His eyes. Our feet are His feet. Our smile is His smile. We are His partners and co-workers.

That spells **inspiration.**

God in Me Inspires Me to Be Me

I think nothing is as **inspiring** as to know that God is at work in our lives. Jesus said, *The Father in me does the work.*[Jn.14:10]

With Him in us, we experience the greatest life on earth. We find a need and meet it. We find a hurt and heal it. We find someone down and lift them up. We find someone who is lost, and show them the way to the light. We find someone discouraged and encourage them.

We are **inspired** by Christ in us.

And we become loving channels of **inspiration** to others.

John said, *If we love one another, God lives in us.*[1Jn. 4:12] That is **inspiring.**

GOD LIVES IN US!

Mother Teresa, of Calcutta, India, could tell us about the **inspiration** of loving people—ministering to the dying and to the poor there on the streets of Calcutta.

Albert Schweitzer could tell us about the **inspiration** of loving people. This distinguished gentleman received over 50 honorary doctorates, besides the many which he earned. He left Europe and invested himself in Africa where he could give hope and care and healing to the poor. To Albert Schweitzer, that was his **inspiration**—his way of loving God.

Chapter 47

SUPREME INSPIRATION

WE HAVE KNOWN the supreme **inspiration** of living and sharing the Jesus life during nearly six decades of global ministry.

To reach out in love and to **inspire** people is the only way to love God. In that way, God lives at our house.[1Jn.4:16]

We constantly do everything we can to spread this love and inspiration to forgotten, neglected people. We share it with everybody we can reach—everywhere we can go.

This book is an outreach **from us to you,** to share the love and the **inspiration** of the Jesus life.

A man from South Africa told us not long ago that a few years before, he had received our books, our tapes and our documentary crusade films—all in the Bantu languages. He had used them as tools to reach and to bless people across South Africa.

He said, "Doctor Osborn, we can safely say that we have already led over 300,000 souls to Jesus Christ through the tools that you have provided for us."

There is nothing more **inspiring** than a Jesus-person who is loving, reaching and lifting people.

The Bangkok Leper

A leper in Bangkok, Thailand, came to our meeting. She lived by a canal in a hovel that she had concocted out of pieces of metal and old boxes.

No one went near her because she was considered to be unclean. She had no friends, but she existed alone, except when she ventured out to beg or to rummage through garbage heaps in search of something to eat.

But God loved her and had a plan for her.

Some way she found out about our crusade and she attended. She secluded herself at the edge of the crowd, under a large tree, where she was less apt to be noticed. She feared lest she might be recognized and chased from the crowd, like she had often been chased from the marketplace.

We shared the Good News of Jesus Christ, of His love and of His death on the cross for us. I explained how God raised Him from the dead, and how He is alive today and wants to come to us to give us His life.

The Good News Inspired Her

To that woman, it was a message of good news. Her hands were drawn and stiff. Her back was bent and she had been unable to straighten up. She suffered excruciating pains in her vertebrae. She could barely walk.

As we led the crowd in prayer, she repeated the prayer, and when finished, she found herself standing erect. Her back was straight. Her spine was completely free. Her hands that had been clenched and stiff were supple again. Her flesh tingled with new life.

She ventured through the crowd and came to the platform where we were calling for the people to tell what God had done for them.

Holding her arms aloft, she said, "Look at my hands. They are free. Look at my flesh. It is clean. I can feel again. There is feeling in all of my body. Look at my back. I can bend over and touch the ground. I can stand up. I could not stand up before."

Inspired by New Friendship

Then she said, "Now Jesus is my friend. I did not know Him before. What you say about Him must be true, because He has healed me. He will come with me to the canal and live with me. When I am sick, He will be with me and heal me."

The woman believed on the Lord Jesus Christ. She was made whole and was forgiven.

What an **inspiration** she was to the multitude of people.

Jesus gave that dear woman self-respect and self-dignity. He came to share His life with her.

No one is too poor. No one is too worthless. Jesus wants to live in you and give you the **inspiration** to touch real life and to share that life with others.

He establishes you in His own class of being, to work with Him, to rule with Him, to plan and to create with Him.

Chapter 48

THE WHY
OF INSPIRATION

WHILE WE ARE here on earth, God has made us His ambassadors to help make everyone else like Him whom we can reach and **inspire** to believe on Jesus Christ.

God's plan concerns one thing on this earth: It is to save people and to inspire them to be like Jesus.

When we have the Jesus life,

1ST **WE EXPERIENCE NEW POWER** in our lives;

2ND **WE REALIZE A BEAUTIFUL CHANGE** that takes place in us;

3RD **WE CONQUER** prejudices;

4TH **WE PREVAIL OVER** fatigue and depression;

5TH **WE RAISE** our achievement level. We become successful;

6TH **WE BREAK OUT** of old habits that have suppressed us;

7TH **WE DEFEAT** worry, fear and anxiety;

8TH **WE GENERATE** enthusiasm and inspiration in the people we touch and influence;

9TH **WE SURMOUNT** handicaps;

10TH **WE IMPROVE** our physical appearance. Where we grew frown wrinkles, we grow smile wrinkles;

11TH **WE MASTER** grief and loneliness;

12TH **WE TRANSFORM** problems into learning processes and convert mountains into plateaus.

The Inspiration of Jesus

Jesus Christ comes to your life to **inspire** you. He says:

"I will make you **beautiful.**

"I will give you **rest.**

"I will give you **peace.**

"I will give you **tranquility.**

"I will give you **faith.**

"I will give you **self-esteem.**

"I will not put you down; I will **lift you up.**"

The Bible says: *If any one is in Christ, he or she is a new creature. Old things are passed away; all things are become new.*2Cor.5:17

267

Why We Are Inspired

What we know is the source of our inspiration.

1. WE ARE INSPIRED by what Jesus did for us.

2. WE ARE INSPIRED because we can receive and assimilate the Jesus life today.

3. WE ARE INSPIRED because we are created in God's image.

4. WE ARE INSPIRED because we are part of God's dream.

5. WE ARE INSPIRED because problems come from Satan, but solutions come from God and we are hooked up with Him.

6. WE ARE INSPIRED because we know that, even though sin separated us from God, He loved us too much to leave us there. Jesus died for us and assumed the punishment and judgment of our sins so that we can be justified before God, as though no sin had ever been committed.

7. WE ARE INSPIRED because all we have to do is believe that God loves us and that Jesus died in our place.

8. WE ARE INSPIRED because Jesus did **enough** in His death on the cross to transform our lives.

9. WE ARE INSPIRED because our sins are already judged in Jesus Christ on the cross.

10. WE ARE INSPIRED because our sicknesses have already been suffered by Jesus, and our guilt is already punished; the price that we ought to have paid was paid by Jesus who loves us.

11. WE ARE INSPIRED because we know that the fight is ended. Our judgment is past when we believe on Jesus. Our sins were judged in Him.

12. WE ARE INSPIRED because the reason for our fear is gone. Nothing stands between us and God now.

13. WE ARE INSPIRED because the reign and the rule of sickness is gone forever from our lives.

14. WE ARE INSPIRED because Satan's authority over us has ended.

15. WE ARE INSPIRED because Jesus is our Lord and our savior, our master, our healer, our deliverer, our source.

As the REST of God **fills** us,

The ZEST of God **thrills** us, and

The BEST of God **builds** us.

God's plan for you is that, when sin is gone, harmony is restored between you and God. You are at one with Him again.

Chapter 49

WONDERS
OF INSPIRATION

THE INSPIRATION of the Jesus life fills you.

1. PERSONAL AMBITION IS GONE. You are **inspired** because you know that God's ambition for you is greater than you ever desired for yourself.

2. HATRED IS GONE. You are **inspired** by His new love. You know that hate never hurt the hated, but only killed the hater. Love is better. It heals the one who is loving, and it heals the one who is being loved.

3. REVENGE AND BITTERNESS ARE GONE. You are **inspired** by the higher influence of the Jesus life. The "eye for an eye," and "tooth for a tooth" principle no longer has appeal. Both parties are **losers.** Inspiring love and patient forgiveness is the new way for you. Both parties are **winners.**

4. LUST AND ABUSE ARE GONE. You are **inspired** by the divine value and dignity of people. You see in another person what God sees in them. Rather than to deprecate or injure them, abuse or use them, you are **inspired** to elevate them, to help them and to lift them. And in doing that, you **lift** yourself.

5. NERVOUSNESS AND HYPERTENSION ARE GONE. You are **inspired** because you know that Jesus is on board your boat, and that He has brought calm to your sea, and life is smooth again.

6. ANXIETY IS GONE. You are **inspired** by the fact that Jesus was never in a hurry, but He was never late. You are on time with Him.

7. RESENTFULNESS IS GONE. You are **inspired** by the fact that, although you may not be able to choose what happens to you, you can choose how you react to it. With Jesus, you grow by every experience because you and Him are winners.

8. JEALOUSY IS GONE. You are **inspired** by realizing and valuing the wonderful self that God made. You are so fulfilled in your relation to Christ and so confident and happy, that there is no one in the world you would rather be than the wonderful **you** that God has made.

9. ENVY AND COVETOUSNESS ARE GONE. You are **inspired** because as God's child, your Father has everything and you have access to it. Is that not terrific?

10. LONELINESS IS GONE. You are **inspired**

because you know that you are now a friend of God and that He is your partner; He lives at your house. You practice the presence of Jesus.

11. EMPTINESS IS GONE. You are **inspired** because you now know that you have purpose and dignity in God's plan. Your life has meaning, for **God,** for **people,** and for **you.** Jesus does His work through you, so you are vital to the world.

12. WEARINESS IS GONE. You are **inspired** because you know you are hooked up with God. You are enthused about life with Him. That enthusiasm is strength, and you draw from it.

13. SICKNESS IS GONE. You are **inspired** by new health because you know that *the life of Christ is manifested in your mortal flesh too.*[2Cor.4:10]

14. YOUR SPIRIT IS REBORN. You are **inspired** by receiving a new kind of life. You accept the Jesus life. You have dignity again. You have purpose and meaning.

15. YOU ARE A SOMEBODY. You are not a NOBODY any more. You are a member of the family of God.

16. YOUR HEART BEATS WITH A NEW RHYTHM. Your nerves are tuned to a new wavelength, God's wavelength of love and peace and life-giving **inspiration.**

17. YOUR MIND IS RENEWED. You think the thoughts of Christ, the things that are true, honest, just, pure, lovely, honorable, virtuous and praiseworthy.[Phil.4:8]

18. YOUR WEAK LEGS STAND UP and walk with God because you no longer cower and crawl in self-reproach, but you march with the strength and comportment of a child of royalty.

19. YOUR BLIND EYES ARE OPEN to see **God** as He is; you see **people** as God sees them, and you see **yourself** as God made you to be.

20. YOUR SHORT LEGS GROW OUT, and walk with a steady stride, the **inspired** stride of a partner with God in kingdom business.

As you look up and see Jesus standing in your boat, you stand up too. You are strong and you grow tall. You are a Jesus-person, with the Jesus life in you to inspire others.

Chapter 50

INSPIRING
POSITIVE DESIRE

A PROSTITUTE was converted in New York City. She had been rough and tough, on dope and a street gang fighter. Her physique was as strong and muscle-bound as a young man.

In a street fight, one of her arms was so mangled that surgeons had to amputate it in order to save her life. Now she wears a prosthesis.

She was transformed by the **inspiring** love of Jesus Christ.

God valued that rough, tough ex-prostitute, and trusted her enough to give Himself to her and to live in her. He needed her to express Himself to others who were unloved.

She became a radiant and an **inspiring** person, with a new zest for life, because she knew she could help other people discover this Jesus.

Together with some other young believers, she began to look for a sharing center where they could tell people about the inspiring life they had discovered in Christ.

Ideal Situation
for Real Inspiration

There were three xxx-rated cinemas side by side in downtown New York. The center one had been closed. This lady longed to use it as a place to witness for Christ. One day a "For Sale" sign was placed on it.

Across the street from the cinemas, there was a flophouse hotel dominated by pimps, their prostitutes and their clients.

It was an ideal situation for demonstrating the love and inspiration of Jesus Christ and to see it blossom in a most beautiful way.

The ex-hooker, with her group, decided to find a way to get the money to buy that cinema.

They succeeded. God miraculously provided, and now it has become a center for sharing the **inspiring** gospel of Jesus, winning and lifting people out of despair into the super lifestyle of Christ.

Admire God's Desire
and Inspire People Higher

That is what God's love means. That is the kind of miracle that can take place when the power of positive desire is inspired by what God desires.

He is standing by your side right now. Draw near to Him. He has sent this message to you. Now, He is ready to give you what you desire from Him.

Nothing is too good for you because you fit into God's plan. He has a purpose for you. So, right now, draw near to Him and pray this prayer, out loud:

PRAYER

Dear Lord, I come to You now, and I receive You into my life. Thank You for Your love that has inspired me to believe that You value me.

My sins are forgiven. My habits are broken. My life is changed.

Today I have been inspired because I see that You created me like You want me to be.

I realize that it was the disobedience of Adam and Eve and unbelief in Your word that condemned me.

But I am so inspired by Your love that never abandoned me.

I am inspired by Your action that saved me, when You died for me.

I am inspired by the redemption that restored me. What You did for me on the cross, I never have to do.

I am inspired by your energy that now endows me. Through Jesus I have found a new life.

I have found the rest of God that fills me.

I have found the zest of God that thrills me.

I have found the best of God that builds me.

I am saved. I am healed. I am Yours. Jesus is in me now.

Thank You for Your life and for Your power. In Jesus' name. AMEN!

The Power of My Desire
(In 60 Seconds)

SINCE I AM created like God and since He is now alive in me, **my DESIRE** for the best in life is **His DESIRE** expressed through me.

*I*t is right for me to desire to **be**, to **have** and to **do** the GOOD that God created me for.

Happiness, **success, health** and **prosperity are** God's original plan for me. He has never changed His mind. **His Love-Plan is my blueprint for Life's BEST.**

My DESIRE is MY FAITH TURNED HEAVENWARD.

I will never allow religious piety and negativism about material blessings **to stifle my desire for God's abundance.** No member of His family is created for **mediocrity** or **poverty.**

I believe that God is **at work in me. I am restored to Him.** Now, my **DESIRE is His DESIRE in me.**

I **believe** in good and **desire** good because I believe in God. **It is right that I enjoy His BEST.**

Dr. T. L. Osborn

THE *MISSION*
OF CHRISTIANITY
OSBORN MINISTRY REVIEW

THE GLOBAL MISSION of Christianity is to witness of Christ and of His resurrection to *the entire world* – to *every creature*.[Mk.16:15] The Apostle Paul said, *Whoever shall call on the name of the Lord shall be saved*.[Rom.10:13]

T.L. and Daisy Osborn shared a worldwide ministry together for over five decades, before her demise in 1995. T.L. resolved to continue his global ministry to multitudes.

The Osborn daughter, Dr. LaDonna, assumed a more visible role in the Osborn world ministries. As the fame of her preaching and teaching ministry has spread, she has increased the influence of the Osborns' gospel expression through her trans-evangelical seminars and mass miracle crusades in new fields of the world such as *Russia*, nations of *French-speaking Africa*, *Eurasia* and the world's largest nation, *China*.

As CEO and Vice-President of *OSFO International* (aka, *OSBORN International*), LaDonna's expertise is making possible the expansion of this ministry in nations around the world. Learn more about the Osborn Global Outreaches through their world wide web, *www. osborn.org*.

The Osborns have reached millions for Christ in nearly a hundred nations during almost six decades. This ministry-brief is included here to inspire young believers that they, too, can carry the *gospel torch into all the world.*Mk.16:15

A Couple Chosen of God

Tommy Lee Osborn and Daisy Marie Washburn were married in Los Banos, California in 1942, at the ages of 17 and 18. Three years later, they became missionaries to India, but were unable to convince the people of ancient, Eastern religions — Muslims and Hindus — about Christ. They had not yet discovered the truths about miracles.

T. L. and Daisy returned to the USA dismayed and disheartened — but not dissuaded. They had not yet discovered that signs, miracles and wonders are essential to convincing *non*-Christian nations about the gospel.

They learned in India that for people of non-Christian nations to believe the gospel, they must see miracle proof that the Bible is true and that Jesus Christ is alive today.

Jesus was...***approved of God** among people by **miracles** and **wonders** and **signs**, which God did by Him in the midst of the people.*Ac.2:22 When T.L. and Daisy were unable to succeed in India, they realized that they needed that same divine *approval* and supernatural confirmation, but they had not yet learned about miracles.

Soon after their demoralizing return to the USA, the Lord appeared to them both, at different times, as they searched for the answer to their dilemma. Then they began to discover the Bible truths that create faith for biblical miracles.

These dynamic truths created in their spirits fresh faith in God's Word. With this new lease on life and having discovered the scriptural facts about miracles, they relaunched their soulwinning saga in 1948 — this time in the Caribbean island-nation of Jamaica.

During thirteen weeks of ministry there, hundreds of biblical miracles confirmed their preaching of Christ and His gospel. Over a hundred deaf-mutes were healed; over ninety totally blind people received sight; hundreds of crippled, paralyzed and lame people were restored; and most important of all, nearly ten thousand souls personally accepted Jesus Christ as their Savior.

Mass Miracle Evangelism

In 1949, after T.L. and Daisy discovered the truths of biblical miracles, and after they returned from Jamaica, they instituted their world evangelism ministry.

They were the ones who pioneered the concept of *Mass Miracle Evangelism* in the era when so-called *"Third World"* nations were mostly *colonized*. T. L. and Daisy addressed audiences of tens of thousands throughout the dangerous years of *nationalism* when foreign political domination was being repulsed by awakening *"Third World"* nations.

Their example inspired national men and women globally, to arise from their restrictive past and to become leading gospel messengers and church builders in the unevangelized nations of the world. Many of them are among the most distinguished and successful Christian leaders known today.

The largest churches in the world today are not in America or Europe. They have been raised up by anointed and gifted national pastors. A single church in Africa seats 54,000 people under one roof, and it is filled three times on Sunday. In another nation, a church is being erected to seat over 60,000 people.

Global Evangelism Concepts

During T.L. and Daisy's unprecedented years as an evangelism team, they have inaugurated numerous programs to reach the unreached. Their concept of *National Missionary Assistance* has resulted in the sponsorship of over 30,000 national preachers as full time missionaries to unevangelized tribes and villages. More than 150,000 new, self-supporting churches have become established globally through the regular assistance provided by the Osborn ministry.

Osborn gospel literature is published in 132 languages. Their *docu*-miracle crusade films, audio and video cassettes, and their digital productions (including Bible courses), are produced in over 70 languages and are circulated globally.

They have provided big airlifts and huge sea-shipments of literature and of soulwinning tools for national gospel ministries abroad. They have provided scores of four-wheel drive vehicles equipped with films, projectors, screens, generators, public-address systems, audio cassettes and cassette players, plus literature for reaching the unreached.

Publishing The Gospel

Dr. Daisy's five major books are *pacesetters* in Christian literature for women — *unique examples of **inclusive** language that addresses both genders.*

T.L. has authored over 20 major books. He wrote his first book, HEALING THE SICK, in 1950. Now in its 47th edition, it is a global favorite, used as a Bible School text book in many nations.

The publisher calls HEALING THE SICK *A Living Classic* — a faith-building best-seller since 1950. Over a million copies are in print and it is now published in *Mandarin* Chinese and is being circulated throughout the world's largest nation, as well as across Russia and many other major nations. It was copied by hand and secretly circulated among suffering people during the long epoch of communist domination.

The Osborns produced a 512 page *Classic Documentary*, **THE GOSPEL ACCORDING TO T.L. AND DAISY.** Nothing else like it has yet been published.

Colonialism
Nationalism
Evangelism

The Osborn daughter, Dr. LaDonna, knows the ministry of World Evangelism. She has lived on the front lines of global soulwinning all of her life — from the days of *colonialism,* through the turbulent years of *nationalism,* and into this 21st century of *mass evangelism and national Church growth.*

The Osborns hold forth these simple truths:

1) That the Bible is as valid today as it ever was,

2) That the divine calling for every believer is to witness of Christ to the unconverted,

3) That every soul won to Christ can become His representative, and

4) That miracles, signs and wonders are what distinguish Christianity from being just another philosophical religion.

To demonstrate these biblical issues is the essence of the Osborns' global *MISSION of Christianity.*

Speaking for Dr. LaDonna and for himself, T.L. quotes Paul: *The ministry we have received of the Lord is to testify the gospel of the grace of God;* [Ac.20:24] *to preach the gospel in the regions beyond.* [2Cor.10:16]

The history of the Osborn ministry is recorded in the historical 24-volume *Encyclo-Biographical Anthology.* It contains more than 23,000 pages, 30,946 photos, 636 *Faith Digest* magazines, 2,024 pages of personal, hand-written diary notes, 1,011 pages of Osborns' news letters, 1,062 pages of unpublished historical data about their world ministry, 2,516 world mission reports, and 6,113 Christian ministry reports.

These 24 giant tomes span over six feet of shelf space and have taken their place in the archives and libraries of institutions of higher learning around the world, including such renowned Universities as Cambridge, Oxford, Oral Roberts University, Regent, Fuller (plus many more in nations abroad), and the archives of many leading denominational headquarters.

Their Global Saga

In T.L.'s eighth decade of life, the Osborn ministry keeps expanding. Following Daisy's demise, T.L. has continued his global evangelism crusades, and his daughter, Dr. La Donna, has expanded her ministries of evangelism and of Church leadership to all five continents as she carries the *torch of the gospel* into this century's new frontiers.

Like the Apostle Paul, LaDonna says, *I am not ashamed of the gospel of Christ, for it is the power of God to salvation to everyone who believes.*Rom.1:16

She believes that *the World is the* **Heart** *of the Church,* and that *the Church is the* **Hope** *of the World.* She contends that without the *World,* the *Church is* **meaningless** and without the *Church,* the *World is* **hopeless**.

The Osborns' passion: *To express and propagate the gospel of Jesus Christ to all people throughout the world.* Their tenet: *No one deserves to hear the gospel repeatedly before everyone has heard it at least once.* Their motto: *One Way – Jesus; One Job – Evangelism.* Their guiding principle: *Every Christian believer – a witness for Christ.*

T. L. and LaDonna Osborns' witness is expressed best by the words of the Apostle John: *We bear record of the Word of God, and of the testimony of Jesus Christ, and of the things that we have seen.*Rev.1:2 *We…testify of these things and have written them: and we know that our testimony is true.*Jn.21:24

"*Listen to me, and you will have a LONG, GOOD LIFE. Carry out my instructions, for they will lead you to REAL LIVING.*" Prov. 4:10,13 Living Bible

"*How excellent is your lovingkindness, O God! ... (to those who) put their trust under your wings. They shall be abundantly satisfied, they shall drink of the river of YOUR pleasure. For with YOU is the fountain of LIFE.*" Psalm 36:7-9

Discover HIS *Good Life.* Live in harmony with God. Get His ideas. Work with His projects. See LIFE as He sees it. Discover who YOU are and YOUR own value. See yourself as God sees you. Live interested in His plans. He believes in YOU and treasures YOUR companionship.

GLOBAL PUBLISHER
OSBORN PUBLICATIONS
P.O. Box 10
Tulsa, OK 74102 USA

✧✧✧

FRENCH DISTRIBUTOR
ÉDITIONS
MINISTÈRES MULTILINGUES
909, Boul. Roland-Therrien
Longueuil, Québec J4J 4L3 Canada

✧✧✧

GERMAN PUBLISHER
SHALOM — VERLAG
Pachlinger Strrasse 10
D-93486 Runding, CHAM, Germany

✧✧✧

PORTUGUESE PUBLISHER
GRACA EDITORIAL
Caixa Postal 1815
Rio de Janiero–RJ–20001, Brazil

✧✧✧

SPANISH PUBLISHER
LIBROS DESAFIO, Apdo. 29724
Bogota, Colombia

(For Quantity Orders, Request Discount Prices.)